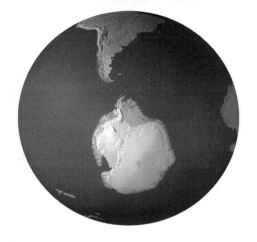

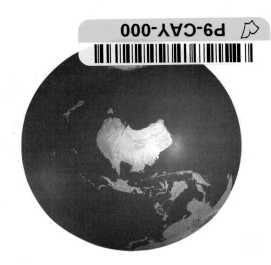

One problem for mapmakers is how to represent
the round Earth on flat paper.
The technique used to do this is called "map projection,"
and there are hundreds of ways to do it.
Each projection has certain strengths.
Each has profound weaknesses.

No single map can give you the full picture
of our amazing and bountiful planet.
If you look at the world from only one vantage point,
you risk missing much.
Our lives are enriched when we begin to see things
from different points of view.

Globe imagery by Oxford Cartographers, Oasis Park, Eynsham, Oxford OX29 4TP, UK. Tel +44 (0)1865 882 884 Fax +44 (0) 1865 882925 Website www.oxfordcarto.com

i

SEEING THROUGH MAPS:
The Power of Images to Shape Our World View

ODT, Incorporated
P.O. Box 134
Amherst MA 01004
1-800-736-1293
1-413-549-1293
FAX: 413-549-3503
E-mail: BAbramms@aol.com

First published and printed in the United States of America in 2001

ISBN 1-931057-00-1

Library of Congress Control Number: 2001090516

Kaiser, Ward L. and Denis Wood

SEEING THROUGH MAPS: The Power of Images to Shape Our World View
1. Cartography-Philosophy, 2. Psychology-Human Perception, 3. Global Studies
I. Kaiser, Ward L. & Denis Wood
II. Title
Includes index

Edited by Bob Abramms
Cover Concept by Ray Seager & Bette Abrams-Esche
Book Design, Layout and Production by Jael Riordan, Boston MA
Cartographic services by FitzGerald Geographics Inc., Amherst MA
Indexing by Marcia Morrison, Prairie Dog Indexing, Lafayette CO

Seeing Through Maps:

The Power of Images to Shape Our World View

Ward L. Kaiser & Denis Wood

Contents

Introduction

This book is based on seven simple assumptions:

- We all use maps.

- Many of us are not particularly good at it.

- Our skills and understanding can be enriched.

- Maps influence us on unconscious levels.

- All maps have their own agenda.

- Discovering the purpose of a map is often the task of the map user.

- When we use maps with greater awareness and competence,
  we will experience heightened satisfaction.

What this book will do is offer facts, perspectives and points of view designed to help you increase the competence you already have. That goal will not be achieved automatically, but we dare to believe that as you immerse yourself in the text and graphics that follow, and as you interact with the ideas presented, you will find your world—almost literally—expanding in new ways.

And, we hope you will have fun in the process, just as we have enjoyed bringing it to you.

THE BOOK IS A MAP

Think of the book you are holding as a map—a road map to the complex, often confusing world of maps. Sounds innocent enough, right?

Nevertheless, it ought to carry a clear warning label:
THIS BOOK MAY BE DANGEROUS TO YOUR CHERISHED VIEW OF THE WORLD.

Of course we are generally comfortable with the views we hold—otherwise we would not hold them, would we? Those views may be naïve or highly sophisticated; the point is, they fit us like our favorite shoes—well-worn and familiar. Why, then, pick up this book, which offers to show us new footwear, which announces at the very outset that it intends to bring about a shift in our views?

Why? Consider the following: see how many of these possibilities intrigue you.

- **Intellectual curiosity**. New ideas are like new products on the market: they come constantly, and they bombard us. Do you often find yourself buying into them uncritically, just as presented? Do you, at the other extreme, regularly reject the unfamiliar as worthless? ("I'll stick with my old shoes, thank you very much.") Or do you let new perspectives s—t—r—e—t—c—h your understanding? Whatever your personal preference and history, here the choice will be yours. As you interact with the pages of this book you will have the satisfaction of tangling with new concepts, new ways of seeing your world.

- **Personal growth.** We, as authors and publisher, have written previously in this field. We have lectured and taught and talked with people times beyond counting. In that process we have seen people develop new attitudes as well as gain factual knowledge. We anticipate that something similar will happen by means of this book. As you participate in dialogue with us, and complete the activities through these pages, your experience of the world will be enriched.

- **Practical application.** You will never look at a map—or at the world that maps depict—the same old way again. That is our promise. You will use maps more effectively, "seeing" what's around you more completely, more accurately. You will better *critique* the messages maps send. No longer will maps be the opaque, sometimes baffling documents they so often are; you will "see through" them. Instead of being a pushover for the map or maps you always assumed were "accurate" or "reliable" or "right," you will have a firmer basis for your own independent judgment. You'll also learn some of the questions to ask about what's left *off* the map, and why.

- **Getting more fun out of life.** Once, one of us took his sons to the Louvre for the experience of viewing "art." Not a good idea. Neither son understood enough to be anything but bored. Today, however, those same let's-get-out-of-here-as-fast-as-we-can, bored-beyond-belief boys enjoy art; they know how to appreciate its many forms. Their lives are richer as a result.

  Many of us approach maps like punishment: we avoid the experience when we can, and when we cannot, we want to get it over with as soon as possible. Our level of comprehension is minimal, so our satisfaction is too.

  Some of you who pick up this book, on the other hand, may not avoid maps; you may be fascinated by them. Perhaps you collect them, or even paper your room with them. We've kept you in mind, too, as we prepared this book. We believe you will gain new information and a deeper appreciation of maps through these pages.

  Wherever you're starting from, before you finish this book we expect you may begin to enjoy maps in a whole new way.

- **Cross-Training.** Many corporations, as well as a number of management consulting firms that serve them, have used some of the maps we will be working with here, in their training sessions. Their goal is not to turn effective executives into amateur cartographers, but to help them grapple with the realization that some of the ideas we have always held may need to be rethought. We call this cross-training; the skills you develop in understanding and using maps will carry over into many other areas of your life. In learning to question the assumptions about the maps you see, we hope you'll also question assumptions hidden within other attitudes, perceptions and beliefs you hold. This book will help you think in new way beyond the confines and borders of your everyday thinking.

If you are like a lot of people, the world of maps is a bit of a maze. Let this book be your guide.
As maps become clearer for you, they may become quite a-maze-ing.

Ward L. Kaiser—Author, *A New View of the World*

Denis Wood—Author, *The Power of Maps*

This book is dedicated to all those who have helped us
expand our view of the world.
And it is dedicated to you, our readers,
who wish to expand your own world view.

Ward L. Kaiser & Denis Wood

Two People, Two Feet Apart

What is the truth? It seems so simple. But when we try to put it into words, it turns out to be much more complex.

Our dictionary says that truth is: "Conformity to knowledge, fact, actuality, or logic." That seems to help until we try to say what "knowledge" is. Or "facts."

"Truth is most commonly used to mean correspondence with facts or with what actually occurred," our dictionary goes on. But when the police officer asks "What happened?" at the scene of even the simplest fender-bender, the officer never hears just one story. If facts were straightforward, we wouldn't need juries to determine them.

The truth can seem awfully slippery at times.

At other times, good sense rebels against such an idea. Of course the truth exists! "We *did* have lunch last Thursday." It is a simple fact.

But is it?

We *did* have lunch last Thursday.

Of course we sat in different chairs and they were sort of angled to the table. Because of this one of us looked at the other against a background of geraniums in coffee cans and birds at a feeder in the dogwood tree; the other against a background of the house next door and thunderhead clouds in the summer sky above it. What at first appears to be one thing—the two of us having lunch—dissolves into two different scenes. Even at a single moment in the meal different things are going on. Sometimes they are so different we can see that the other person's eyes have drifted from the table. Ward has moved his eyes to something going on in the tree behind Denis, or Denis has moved his eyes to something happening in the driveway behind Ward. We have to reorient ourselves to the reality of the other by turning our chairs to face each other more squarely.

Sometimes one of us sees something the other misses completely: a bird at the feeder (gone by the time the other turns), or a kid maneuvering on a skateboard (and the other turns, but he is too late). Then one

2

person's experience of lunch includes that event. The other's doesn't.

These differences in the experience of lunch result from a space less than than a foot or two between our chairs and a difference in orientation of maybe 90°. We can add to this our different backgrounds, different professions, different styles of thinking, and all the rest. Then, despite everything we share, it becomes hard to say—even of this simple meal—precisely and unanimously what was what. This is true even *in the moment*, much less in the mind, or in the memory a day, a week, a month later or even longer.

But, *dammit!* We did have lunch together.

Sure, okay, if that's all you want to say: we had lunch.

There may *be* something we can call the truth if we keep it so simple it doesn't really matter.

Two Peoples, a World Apart

Two people, two feet apart. What if they had been two peoples a world apart? What if they had been inhabitants of New York and Beijing contemplating the U.S. bombing of the Chinese embassy in Belgrade?

If all we can say of the truth is that bombs fell on a building we might as well say nothing. Because it is not about that. That's *past*. It is about now and tomorrow. It is about who (if anyone) will apologize to whom. It is about what was really going on, and if this was a sign, what was it a sign of, and is it reasonable to have bombs? It is about what life means if it can end this way. It is about stuff like that.

"It's hot out here," one says.

"It sure is," says the other.

"It's from global warming," says the first, "too many cars."

"Bullshit!" says the second.

It was easy to agree about it being hot, but attributing the heat to the cars implies a course of corrective action. That raises the stakes. Suddenly it is a matter of perception. Is it *really* hotter than it used to be? Or is this a *perspective* effect? If it is hotter, is this *usual* or *unusual*? If unusual, did *people* cause it? If we did, *what* can we do about it now?

Going back to our first example, you might ask, "Well, what about someone across the street watching the two of you having lunch? Wouldn't they have an *objective* view? What about the UN perspective on the bombing? What does *science* have to say about global warming?"

And, yes, each has its truth too, but there are three truths now instead of two. Three truths . . . *or more*. The UN scarcely speaks in a single voice, and in the case of science speaking about global warming we're talking about dozens and dozens of truths.

How many can we stand?

How do we act if we don't know what's true? Isn't life hard enough already without adding to it the uncertainty of there being many truths?

Frankly, life is hard enough already without pretending it is so simple there is only a single truth.

Maps Are Descriptions Too

What does this have to do with maps?

Maps are descriptions of the way things are. They are a lot like the answers people give police at the

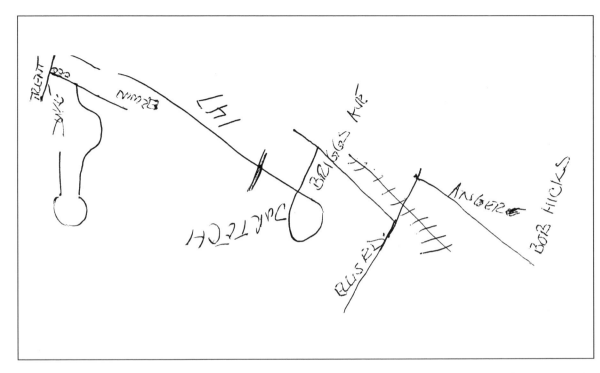

Figure 1. *We were lost. A security guard at Duke University in Durham, North Carolina, drew this map of the best way to get from Duke to Angier Avenue. (1993).*

together to form a sequence of instructions: "Get off 147 at the Briggs Avenue exit just past Durham Tech," is what the map says, "and where Briggs dead ends, turn right . . ."

Is it true? As a matter of fact it got us exactly where we wanted to go, so it was true enough. It need not have been true. The guard could have been irritated by our presence and drawn a map intended to mislead us. (People have been known to do such things.) Or the guard could simply have been mistaken about which street went where.

Is his map complete? It is complete *enough*. It is not a complete map of Durham. It is not even a complete map of Durham streets. But it included everything we needed to get from Duke to Angier Avenue.

How accurate is it? Again, it is accurate enough for the purpose. As a matter of fact, Angier Avenue *doesn't* "T" into Ellis Road. It crosses it. But this didn't matter if we were following the map.

Is it precise? Not very. On one part of the map an inch equals a couple of hundred yards. On another it equals a couple of miles. But again, it was precise enough for us!

The guard's map perfectly fulfilled its purpose. The guard managed this by selecting from everything he knew about Durham only what was necessary to his purpose: to guide us where we wanted to go.

scene of an accident. Questions of truth are never far away.

We can ask the same things about maps that we ask about any description. How true? How complete? How accurate? How precise?

The answers depend on our purposes, or what we need the description for.

Figure 1 is the map a guard made to show us how to get from Duke University, in Durham, North Carolina, to an auto repair shop on Angier Avenue. It brings institutions (Duke, Durham Tech), roads (NC 147, Briggs Avenue), and landmarks (a bridge, the railroad tracks)

4

All Maps Are Selective

Every map is a purposeful selection from everything that is known, bent to the mapmaker's ends. Every map serves a purpose. Every map advances an interest.

This is easy to see in a map like the one we have been looking at which was drawn with the special purpose of helping us visualize instructions: "It's kind of complicated," the guard had said as he put pen to paper. It is not so easy to see the purpose in an ordinary map of the world like our next example.

A world map like the one in Figure 2 seems to have no special purpose. Or it may seem to be ready to serve any purpose you might bring to it. For this reason such maps are often called "general purpose maps" in an effort to differentiate them from "special purpose maps" like the one the guard drew. But as we will see, there are no general purpose maps. Every map serves a specific purpose. Every map advances an interest.

We should have put "world map" in quotation marks. Although this is how we talk about maps like this (we *call* them "world maps"), this is no more a map of the world than the guard's was a map of Durham.

How else to call such a map? No other name is quite as convenient, and everyone calls it a world map, so we will too. But, as we do, we're going to keep in mind that a great deal is missing. *Often what's missing is a clue to the purpose the map is serving.*

In this case, both of the earth's poles are missing. Much of Antarctica is missing too. So are all signs of relief: there are no mountains, valleys or plains, either on the land or beneath the sea. There is no atmosphere. Certainly there are no clouds. For that matter there is no sign of life, either vegetable or animal. There is no sign of human life either, no countries, no Cairo, New York or Mexico City, no Great Wall of China.

It is hardly, in other words, the world. So what is it?

At first thought it may seem to be a map of land and water. But when you think about it, too much water

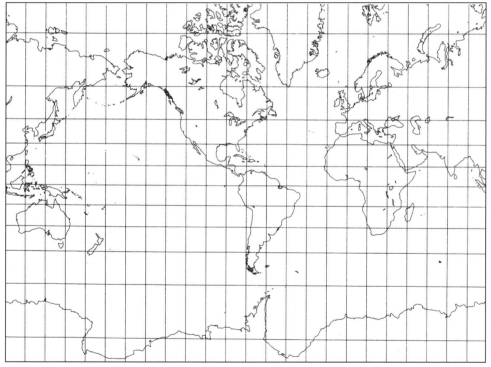

Figure 2 *This is a modern outline reconstruction of the 1569 map on which Gerardus Mercator introduced his famous projection. Notice the way the rectangles forming the grid get longer and longer as you move toward the North and South Poles. A redrawn version of his actual map is on page 6.*

lies on the land in the form of ice for this to be a map of water. There are literally thousands of tons of water in the ice that lies over Antarctica and Greenland. Tons of water exist in the atmosphere too. So it is not a map of land and water. The map has to be about something else.

As with the truth, the subject of the map seems simple. But when you try to put it into words, it turns out to be hard. In fact, the map is not at all what it seems. Even in its updated form (see page 4) the map is actually still a piece of history. It reminds us that when it was made, people crossed oceans in sailing ships. A good description of this map's subject would be, "Places where ships will float and places where they won't." This still isn't *quite* right. Even modern ice-breakers get stuck in the solid ice of the Arctic Ocean. Sailing ships never got into that ice at all.

All Maps Have a Purpose

The sailable world is what this map is paying attention to. It is a map for a world of sailors. It should not surprise us, then, that the way the map shows the world reflects the interests of sailors too. The map on page 6 is a modern redrawing of one Gerhardus Mercator made in 1569. He called his map, "A New and Enlarged Description of the Earth With Corrections for Use in Navigation." His title was very precise about the map's purpose, and right over North America he engraved a long description of how he made it.

We will have much more to say about this map further on. What's important here—where we are concerned with the *purposes* maps serve—is what Mercator's map was *for*. The map made it possible for sailors to draw a straight line to their destination and sail along it. Any straight line drawn on Mercator's map is a line of constant compass bearing. You'd draw a line to your destination, set your compass to the bearing of the line, follow it and, making allowances for winds and tides, get where you wanted to go.

Mercator's work was not appreciated immediately. For one thing, the map was too different at a time when sailors put a great deal of faith in tradition. For another, the map was too small to be of much practical use. It wasn't until the ideas behind Mercator's map became understood and accepted, and until the map was redrawn as a series of regional sea *charts*, that his work became popular.

In the 18th century when world travel became more common, so did the use of Mercator's map. In that increasingly scientific age the map's technical practicality gave it great authority. It was in the 18th century that Mercator's map began to be seen as *the* world map, essentially because it was *the* map of the seaman, *the* map of the navigator, *the* map of the professional world traveler. As Western nations made themselves into colonial powers, Mercator's map of the world came to be seen as an important icon of Western superiority.

> **CHARTS:** A chart is a map designed for navigation. There are coastal charts, harbor charts, nautical charts for use at sea, and aeronautical charts for flying.

6

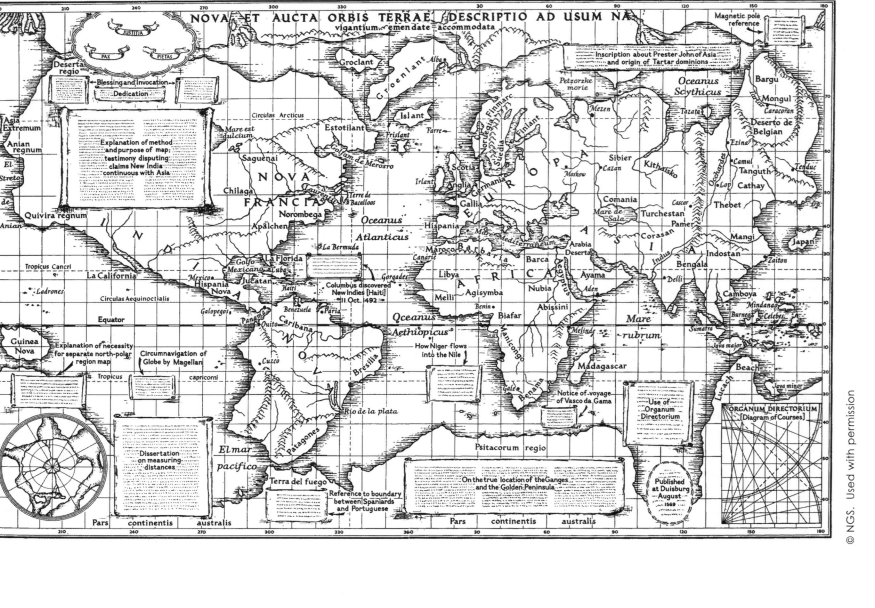

Figure 3. *This is a redrawing of the map Gerardus Mercator published in 1569 to present his new projection. The original is too hard to reproduce. The title reads, in English, 'A New and Enlarged Description of the Earth With Corrections for Use in Navigation.' Its intended use could not be more clearly spelled out.*

A Map's Quality Is Related To Its Purpose

The Mercator as an icon of Western superiority is something else we will have much to say about further on. Here our point is that this famous, popular, and apparently "general purpose" map of the world turns out to have been created to serve a very special purpose, one almost as special as the purpose served by the security guard's map. In fact, both maps have similar purposes. Both are about helping you get where you want to go.

How "true" is the Mercator? Many people think it is not very true. To see what they are talking about, do this: hold the modern version of the Mercator up to a globe. It is obvious there that Mexico is larger than Alaska, but on the Mercator it looks as though Alaska is three times the size of Mexico. On the globe you can see that Africa is significantly larger than North America, but on the Mercator it is the other way around. On the globe South America can be seen to be almost twice as large as Europe, but on the Mercator Europe seems to be larger than South America.

The proportions of places on the globe are *not* the proportions shown on the Mercator. On the Mercator, places closer to the north and south poles are proportionally larger—often much larger—than places closer to the equator.

How should we think about this? Our dictionary says that to distort something is, "to twist out of a proper or natural relation of parts," and in this simple, straightforward sense Mercator's map distorts the sizes of places on the globe. But the dictionary goes on to say that to distort is "To cast false light on, alter misleadingly, misrepresent." In this second sense, the "twisting out of a proper relation" is intended to *mislead*. The problem is that these two senses of "distort" are often confused.

Does the Mercator mislead? It so happens that it is *impossible* to make compass bearings straight lines on

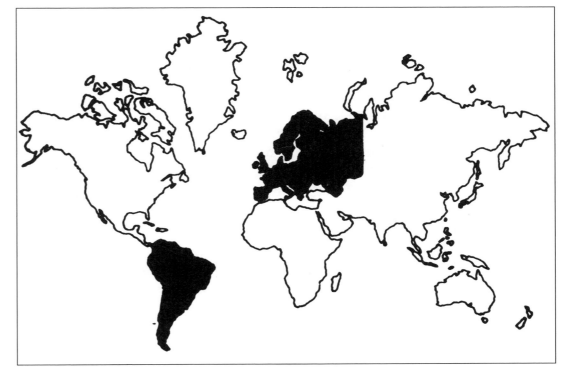

Figure 4. *The Mercator projection makes Europe look larger than South America. In fact, Europe has only 3.8 million square miles and there are 6.9 million square miles in South America. Of course, the projection was never designed to facilitate the comparison of areas.*

8

a map that also gives places their proper proportions. To show the one, the other *has to be* "twisted out of a proper relation of parts." No map can show both of these things together.

To show one truth you have to distort another. This is one good reason we need so many truths.

In our case this is because a world map is a two-dimensional image of a three-dimensional globe. There simply is *no way* to "squash" the globe into a plane without losing something "true" about the globe. Think about the way you can run your finger around and around the globe. You can't do this on the Mercator simply because of its edges. This is a crude illustration, but it gets to the heart of the matter: the map is not the globe.

What this means is that every map is a *view* of the globe. From this perspective, different maps are much like the different views the two of us had of our lunch together; different because we were focused on different but equally valid things. Different maps are like telling a story, but from different points of view.

Another way of saying this is that different maps show different selections from what is available in a medium where you cannot show everything at once. What was true about the map the guard at Duke made is true about all maps: *all maps are selections from everything that is known, bent to the mapmaker's purpose.*

Because it was not part of Mercator's purpose to give the proper proportions of places on the globe, it is not fair to imply that his map intends to cast a false light on, or misleadingly alter them. The loss of proportionality was an *unavoidable consequence* of Mercator's purpose to make compass bearings straight lines. This loss of proportionality, most serious in the

infrequently traveled polar regions, was of no practical importance for sailing, just as the lack of proportionality in distances on the guard's map was of no practical importance for us.

Furthermore, when the Mercator was applied in a series of regional sea charts as intended, the distortion was greatly reduced. *Mercator's purpose was to help sailors plot their courses across the ocean, and for that purpose his map worked.*

It still does.

As people require more than one truth, so sailing requires more than a single view of the world. As useful as the Mercator is, it could not be used for navigation by itself. No single map could ever suffice. For one thing, no map of the world could ever be sufficiently detailed for the careful sailing required to take a ship along a coast, or in and out of a harbor. For that purpose navigators had lockers filled with local charts. For another thing, no navigator could use the Mercator to plot his *shortest* route. For that purpose he needed a map that shows **great circles** as straight lines.

Showing great circles as straight lines is another thing maps can do—but *not* a map that makes compass bearings straight lines, or that gives areas their proper proportions. This is another example of the fact that all maps are selections from everything that is known, bent to the mapmaker's purpose. Like telling a story from different points of view, each purpose requires a different map.

GREAT CIRCLE: This is any line that, like the equator, divides a sphere into two equal halves. The shortest distance between any two points on a sphere is part of a great circle.

What *is* a great circle? It is any line that divides a sphere into two equal halves. The *equator* is a great circle. It divides the globe into northern and southern hemispheres. While the shortest distance between two points on a plane is a straight line, the shortest distance between two points on a sphere is part of a great circle. This is just another of those differences between planes and spheres that complicates the world of maps.

You may already know about great circle *routes*. Take another look at a globe. If you were to fly from New York to Beijing would you head east over the Atlantic, Europe and all of Asia? Or west across the U.S. and the Pacific? Or would you fly north, more or less over the pole?

As you can see (and, if you want to make sure, you can use a piece of thread or string to measure it), the shortest route (by far!) goes close to the North pole. This is a great circle route, a segment of a circle which, if it were continued, would circle the globe and, like the equator, divide it in two.

As you can also see, flying along the great circle route from New York to Beijing would require constantly changing your bearing. First you would be flying approximately north, then west, then south.

The way navigators work is to plot their route on a map that shows great circle routes as straight lines. They can do this on a kind of map called **gnomonic**. Such maps do not have a lot of other useful characteristics, so they are not used much. Since great circles are almost straight on **Lambert conformal conic** maps, these are increasingly used for this purpose, especially for aeronautical charts.

Having laid out their route on such a map, the pilots transfer it to a Mercator. Here they approximate the route with a chain of straight line segments. They then fly along these segments which, since they are straight lines on a Mercator, are lines of constant compass

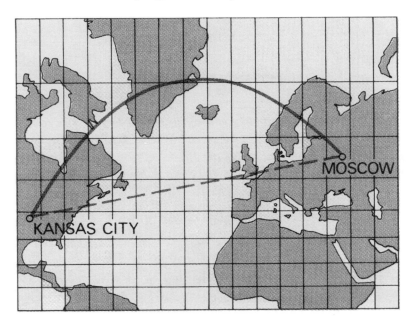

Figure 5. *Mercator's projection showing the line of constant compass bearing (straight) and the great circle route (curved) between Kansas City and Moscow. Although it shows up as longer on this projection, the great circle route is shorter on the globe. A composite line composed of little short lines of constant compass bearing would then be fitted to the great circle route. These are what a pilot would follow.*

GNOMONIC: This is a kind of map that shows great circles as straight lines.

LAMBERT CONFORMAL CONIC: This is a kind of map on which great circles are close enough to straight lines to make it useful for aeronautical charts.

bearing. This is similar to how ships navigate too. Of course today this is all done by computers.

10

To Repeat: A Map's Quality Is a Function of Its Purpose

Would it be fair to say Mercator's world map *lied* because it lacked detail about the coasts and harbors?

Not really. If you want to show the world's 197 million square miles on a chart that's twelve feet square, some details are going to be left out. It is like telling a story. If someone wants it told in 60 seconds, the details that would make it last an hour have to go. You just hit the main points. This isn't lying. (It is not incompleteness either.) When mapmakers just hit the main points, ignoring, say, all the tiny twists and turns of a coastline, they call it *generalization*.

> **GENERALIZATION:** When mapmakers smooth out coastlines or take the kinks out of rivers to give the general idea, as when they are showing the whole Mississippi or the whole East Coast of North America.

Similarly, Mercator's failure to give places their proper proportions doesn't amount to lying, nor is it fair to think about it as inaccurate. The changes in proportionality are smooth, continuous and predictable. They are necessary consequences of the manipulations Mercator had to carry out in order to make compass bearings straight lines.

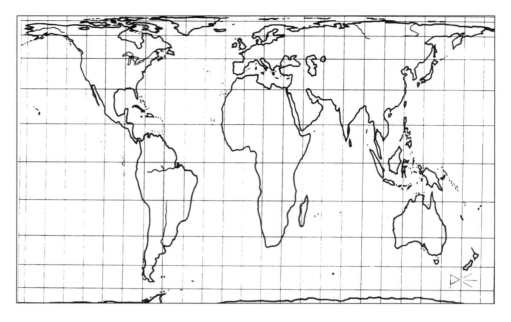

Figure 6. *What a different world this seems to be. This is a projection of the world that gives areas their true relative size. You can easily see how much larger South America is than Europe. On the other hand, compass bearings are not straight on this map. Maps really are like points of view.*

To make all this clearer, take a look at the map above. What a different world!

This is called the Peters map, named for Arno Peters who introduced it in 1974. Unlike Mercator whose purpose was to help sailors, Peters' purpose was to help the rest of us. Peters believed that widespread use of Mercator maps for purposes that had nothing to do with navigation, built up in our minds a seriously distorted image of the world.

It is fair to say Peters was especially concerned about our image of Africa and the countries close to the equator that were given short-shrift as a conse-

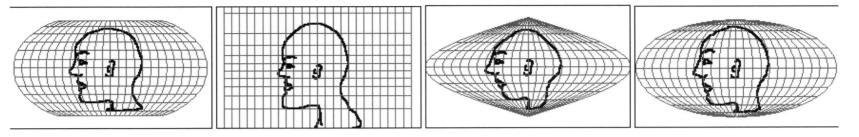

Figure 7. *A head drawn on one projection (Robinson's) has been transferred to the Mercator (center left) and a sinusoidal (center right) and finally to a Mollweide (far right). The 'natural' profile could have been drawn on any of these and then plotted on the others. This is just a way of getting a sense of what different projections do.*

quence of the Mercator projection. On a Mercator the former Soviet Union is much larger than Africa. Since size can often imply importance, wouldn't people looking at such a map imagine that the Soviet Union was much more important than Africa?

Africa is actually about the same size as the former Soviet Union and the United States combined. Africa is *substantially larger* than the United States and the current Russia. If size were what mattered, Africa would rank second in importance only to Asia. Europe would compete with Australia for last place. There is no question that the Peters makes this much more evident than the Mercator.

Which map is right?

They're both right. They're just "right" about different things. But again, they're both "wrong," too.

Try this exercise! Focus on the shapes of the continents. First hold the Peters up next to a globe. Is Africa really so tall and skinny? Is Alaska so stringy? The shapes on the Peters are precisely as distorted as sizes on the Mercator. Good shape, what mapmakers call

conformality, is one of the things Peters had to sacrifice to keep the areas of places in proper proportion.

On the other hand, the Mercator does show true shapes. This is something we will have more to say about later on, but if you compare shapes on the Mercator with those on the globe you will see that if shapes are true, they are true in a very peculiar way.

> **CONFORMALITY:** This is the ability of a map to preserve angular relationships as they exist on the globe. What this means is that the map can show shapes the way they are. A conformal map cannot show areas in their true size.

In fact, shapes are only locally true on the Mercator. That is, shapes are true in this little spot here and in that little spot there. Because sizes change so drastically, when you look at something as large as a continent you have one small true shape toward the equator (say Mexico), and another small true shape near the North pole (say Alaska), but the latter is so many times larger than the former, that when you put them together, the shape of North America as a whole is not right.

It's as if you were to draw a picture of someone's face, and you got the shape of the chin right, and you got the shape of the forehead right, but you made the forehead ten times larger than the chin. Then even though every part was right, the shape of the whole face would seem to be wrong.

Shapes get truer and truer the more you zoom in on the Mercator. This is why the Mercator is so widely used today for mapping small areas in great detail.

Each Map Has Its Own Point of View

So which map should you use?

You should use the map that best serves your purpose. Only when you are given a map's purpose, can the map's rightness—its truth—be assessed.

If you're flying across the ocean, the Mercator is going to be useful, but if you're trying to compare the relative size of places you will want to use the Peters. If you're trying to find your way from Duke to Angier Avenue, neither will be the slightest help.

We need a local point of view to get across town. We need a comparative perspective to get sizes right. We need the point of view of a compass to fly across the ocean.

Every map takes a point of view. No map can show everything at once, any more than the two of us could see the same things at the same time at our lunch together. At the very least, if we were to see each other, we couldn't see ourselves! Besides, sometimes one of us was in the kitchen getting the coffee, or visiting the bathroom. Then our experiences of the meal were sharply divided. One of us might ask, "Remember that bird a while ago that—" and the other will say, "No, I was in the kitchen getting the coffee, but you told me about it." Yet we did have lunch together.

The map that is, as it were, getting the coffee (making compass bearings straight) can't be sitting on the porch taking in the scene (showing places in their proper proportions). Yet there is only one planet.

It takes many different eyes to see it all, and many different maps to show it. That this is a strength, not a weakness, is what the rest of this book is about.

Questions

Q: Is there such a thing as a true and accurate map?

A: No, not in any final sense. Maps are merely descriptions of the world (or part of it) from a particular perspective or bias.

Q: How do I figure out what's left off a map?

A: One important clue is to look at what is at the center. Sometimes what is not important to the mapmaker is put off to the edges, or left out altogether. Ask questions like:

- What would a sociologist, anthropologist or psychologist include on this map?
- To what extent does the map reflect commercial interests (like showing restaurants and gas stations) or highlight recreational and aesthetic information (like hiking trails and vistas)?
- What can I discern about the self-interest of the mapmaker and/or those who commissioned the work? How do you suppose that self-interest or agenda may have influenced choices of what to include or omit?

Q: Why do I have to care about all these complicated words like: great circle, Gnomonic, Lambert conformal conic, generalization and conformality?

A: Well, you don't. But they ARE the precise terms used to describe certain features or characteristics about a map. There won't be a quiz on the terms (at least not from us!), but at the same time there is no need to be intimidated by the words just because they are new to you.

Maps Preserve Descriptions, Maps Can Be Moved Around

There are as many ways of making maps as there are truths to map.

Maps are descriptions of the way things are, descriptions made to support the human purposes that summon the maps into being. Depending on the purpose, you can make a highly useful map with no more than a pencil and a piece of paper.

Even today people are as likely to hand-draw maps as they are to make them with computers. It is important to keep in mind that it is not how the map is made that makes the map. It is not the degree of detail, nor the quality of the printing, nor the name of the government agency stamped in its corner. *The value of the map is the degree to which it serves its purpose.*

It is because this is *so important* that we first looked at the guard's map of the route to Angier Avenue. For its purpose the map was perfect. Could it have been any simpler?

Actually, yes: it would have been simpler for the guard to have sketched the route in the air with gestures of his hands, or to have scratched it on the ground with his foot.

Unfortunately the map sketched in the air would have disappeared as it was being made; and we could not have carried the one scratched on the ground away with us. Neither of these "maps" would have been in hand when we spiraled down the off-ramp from NC 147, disoriented as we so often are when exiting a freeway.

Can we call gestures made in the air maps? What about scratches made on the ground?

Like maps, they *are* descriptions of the way things are, but since they aren't permanent or portable, they have no long range use. Maps are *graphic objects* that *preserve* descriptions so that these descriptions can be used at other times and places.

This is what the guard's map did. It put the knowledge about Durham that the guard had accumulated over his lifetime at our disposal in a form we could carry away with us and consult when we needed to.

Mercator's map did the same thing. It took knowledge about the world that people had been gathering for millennia and put it in a form that sailors could sail away with and use when they needed to.

Peters' map pulled together what people have learned about the relative size of places and put that in a form that people anywhere could turn to at will.

This is the power of maps, to make useful descriptions of the way things are available to others in other times and places.

Everyone Can Make a Map

Professional mapmaking texts are filled with instructions on how to make the more or less permanent graphic objects we call maps. Such knowledge is obviously useful. But as you know from your own experience—and from the story of the guard—all you really need is a pencil and a piece of paper.

There are no rules for making maps. There is no right way, no wrong way. If you are making a map for your own purposes and do not care who else can read it—or do not *want* anyone else to be *able* to read it—the map need not even be intelligible to others.

On the other hand if you are making a map of a well known place and want others to recognize it, intelligibility *is* an issue. In this case making marks others will respond to, and putting them together to make a whole that others will recognize, is essential.

But again there is no *special* set of marks or symbols you have to use to do this.

The marks and symbols mapmakers use are the same as those artists and advertisers use. They are the same ones teachers use when they are writing on the chalkboard.

Not only are the symbols common but there is an enormous variety of them. Think, for a moment, about the many kinds of maps you are familiar with. Local street maps use one set of symbols; highway atlases and gas station maps use another. Few of these symbols are the same as those on the maps in reference atlases, and there is another set altogether used by the US Geological Survey. The maps that appear on television, in the daily newspaper and in weekly news magazines are different still. Sometimes these use pictures like those on the tourist maps you occasionally find under your plate in roadside restaurants, or the maps you get at amusement parks. The marks and symbols on maps in children's books are another story, and so are those in books of fantasy and science fiction. Electoral precinct (or political riding) maps, maps of school districts, bus maps, flood plain maps, and the maps made by planning departments for public hearings have a different character still.

These are a lot of examples. They demonstrate the enormous variety of maps in our everyday world.

As different from each other as these maps may be, it is interesting to note how little trouble you have moving from one of them to another. This shows how flexible and adaptable maps are. Though special knowledge may be required to help you make some of these maps, for others no special knowledge is required at all. The conventions used in making intelligible marks and assembling them into recognizable wholes are the same conventions used to sketch a map for a game of

Pictionary, to write a note, to tell a story, lay out a scene, or even just to talk. (See Figure 8 to the right)

This may be obvious in the case of the guard's sketch map. But here (as Figure 9, below) is a map of the world made precisely the same way; yet it includes some very sophisticated geographical notions.

This map was drawn by a Duke University student taking an introductory geography course. The shapes of the continents make it fairly certain the student had been studying a Mercator map. The map differentiates six categories of surface, and among other things shows ocean currents, trade routes, and land and water bridges.

Figure 8. *Someone drew this map to illustrate the word 'foreign' in a game of Pictionary. The rhetorical skills involved here, of organization and presentation, are the same that are needed to make more elaborate maps like the one to the lower left.*

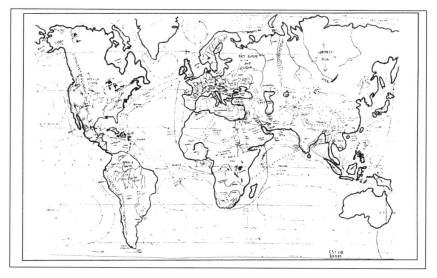

Figure 9. *Mark Fisher, a Duke student, drew this map in 1995 as part of a final exam in an introductory geography course. The distortions in size and shape suggest that he had been studying a Mercator projection. Drawing on the same skills used to make the crude Pictionary sketch, above right, this sketch map is a sophisticated and detailed image of the world.*

Our point is that this map was made the same way the guard's map was, with a pencil and a piece of paper.

None of this is to say that the technical considerations we touched on in our first chapter are not important. Things like conformality and generalization *are* important, but they become *critical* only in certain kinds of maps. This is true about map projections too. If you're sketching a map to help someone find your house, you don't need to worry about map projections. But if you're drawing a map to illustrate the relative size of Africa and North America, then the projection you use—implicit or otherwise—is very important. In this case, it makes all the difference in the world.

As we said at the beginning of this chapter, it all depends on your purpose.

Maps of the Whole Globe Call for Map Projections

Most maps are plans. That is, they are maps of areas so small that they might as well be flat. The guard's map is a plan. So are the maps in your local newspaper of neighborhoods and roads. Even your state or provincial highway map may be a plan.

So, however, is the Duke student's map of the world. The student's map shows that plans don't have to be limited to local places.

People made maps of the world as plans for millennia—even after it became common knowledge that the earth was a sphere. The plan form was traditional, or it was convenient, or it was fun.

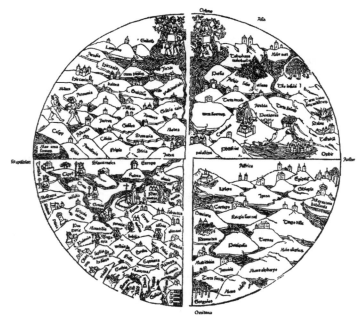

Figure 10. *With the exception of some simple sketches this is the first printed map of the world. It dates from 1475. It illustrated a book,* Rudimentum Novitiorum. *The English title is* The New Beginning *It was really the end of this idea of the earth. Columbus would sail into the Caribbean not a generation later, and shortly after that Vasco da Gama would round the Cape of Good Hope. But the form was traditional and habits change slowly.*

Although people still make plan maps of the world, today the image of a *projected* map stands behind almost all of them, precisely as Mercator's map stood behind the map the Duke student drew.

In the student's case, the inspiration of Mercator may have been unconscious. It may have come from memories the student carried in his head of projected maps seen since childhood, in textbooks and on classroom walls, in advertisements and on logos, on coffee mugs and hanging behind the commentators on the evening news.

Unconscious or not, implicit or otherwise, every map of the whole world *has to be a projection*. Projection is the only way to show the surface of a sphere on a surface that is flat.

We all have an idea of what projection is: light shines through—or off—one surface, casting its image onto another. It's how slide projectors, opaque projectors, and overhead projectors work.

An easy way to think about map projection is to imagine the projector bulb *inside* the globe, with the screen wrapped around the globe to make a cylinder. Once you've traced the image the globe projects onto the screen, you can cut the screen anywhere—it is a cylinder—and let it unroll.

Presto! Flat map of spherical globe. Incidentally, an example of a cylindrical projection is the Mercator.

You can project the globe onto anything that will roll out flat when you cut it.

A sphere will not do this. Think about a basketball. It will not roll out flat when you cut it. Half a basketball is only a *little* flatter than a whole basketball. If you try to flatten half a basketball, parts are always popping up. Only if you cut the basketball into little pieces, will they lie flat. But then there is nothing left of the sphere! (You have a bunch of individual little plan maps instead.)

A cone will lie flat when you cut it, so you can project the globe onto a cone. Or rather onto *cones*, because it is hard to project the whole globe onto a single cone. You can even project a part of the globe onto a plane.

These are the three main types of projections: cylindrical, conic, and plane.

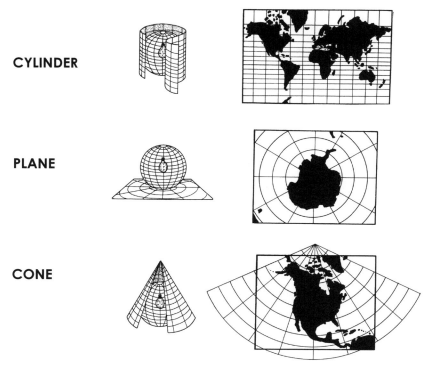

CYLINDER

PLANE

CONE

Figure 11. *You can project the globe onto anything that will roll out flat when you cut it. Planes, cones and cylinders are most common. Note the effect each has on the pattern made by the lines of latitude and longitude.*

This is the *idea*. However, projections are not actually made this way. Projections are made mathematically. Instead of literally projecting each point on the earth's surface onto a plane, each point on the earth's surface is *assigned* to a point on the plane by a mathematical formula.

The formula, as it were, takes the place of the rays of light that would have been involved in a literal projection.

What projection amounts to is figuring out the image the **graticule** will make on the flat map.

The graticule is what we call that network of parallels and meridians with which we imaginatively cloak the globe. The graticule is that grid of latitude and longitude lines that includes the equator, the Tropics of Cancer and Capricorn, the Arctic and Antarctic Circles, the Greenwich Meridian, and, of course, all the rest of them.

Figure 12 *The graticule is the name mapmakers give to the network or mesh of lines that cloaks the globe. North-south running lines are meridians. We count them 180º east and west from the Greenwich, or zero, meridian. These are degrees of longitude. East-west running lines are parallels. We count them 90º north and south to the poles from the equator. These are degrees of latitude. It's jargony, but it's simple.*

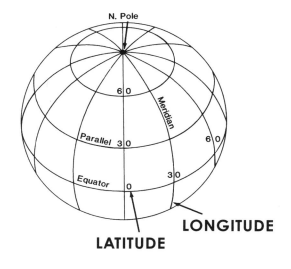

20

If you can imagine the projector bulb inside a globe that is just made out of these lines, and imagine the graticule getting finer and finer, turning into a mesh—*that's* what's being projected by the formulas.

What you end up with, really, is a list of the global coordinates (so many degrees of longitude east or west, so many of latitude north or south) and their projected *x, y* coordinates on the paper (so many inches up, so many inches over).

Different formulas "project" the graticule onto the plane differently, and different projections preserve, or present, different characteristics of the graticule. The problem is that spheres and planes can't be transformed into each other without stretching or shrinking or tearing or wrinkling.

Think about that basketball. Or an orange. "When you peel an orange, you can understand why it's so hard to draw the earth," Nigel Holmes, mapmaker for *Time* magazine, writes, "The peel won't lie flat. Map projection is the science of wrestling the orange peel into submission."

Or try the opposite. Try to wrap a flat piece of paper or cloth (which would be the plane or map) around a ball (the sphere or earth). You *can* do it, but what about all that extra cloth gathering here, the extra paper crumpling there? What are you going to do about *that*?

Now imagine cutting the excess off and trying to flatten the cloth or paper. It will have holes wherever you cut the excess off.

If you want to wrap up the globe in a piece of paper, the paper has to have holes in it; it has to be cut.

This is how the everyday globes you know are made. The paper on which the flat map is printed is cut

into twelve "gores." "Gore" is a technical term mapmakers borrowed from dressmakers. In dressmaking a gore is a tapered piece of cloth used in a skirt, or to make an umbrella. It is also one of the sections of a map that is glued to the surface of a sphere to turn it into a globe. Even with the sheet cut up as we see in Figure 13, there is still wrinkling and puckering that has to be ingeniously patched over.

It is a simple fact of nature. *It does not matter if you are doing it physically or mathematically: to wrap a plane around a sphere or to flatten a sphere into a plane, something has to give.*

By "something has to give" we mean that some characteristic of how things are on the globe has to be given up—lost—in the transformation to the plane.

Earlier we pointed out that you can run your finger around and around the globe. This is something you

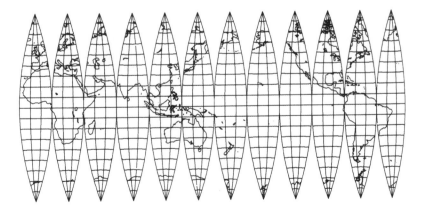

Figure 13. *To make a globe with these gores you would paste them along the equator and then carefully smooth the gore sections into place. The material cut away allows the paper to lie more or less smoothly on the globe. Even so there will be some stretching of the paper, and unavoidable wrinkling and puckering.*

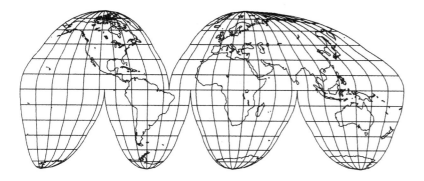

Figure 14. *This is Goode's homolosine projection. It is an equal-area projection invented by John Paul Goode in 1923. In some sense it represents the opposite of the gore map on page 20. This would be one way of 'unfolding' the surface of the sphere to make it lie flat.*

can't do on Mercator's map, where you run into an edge. This connectedness that is characteristic of the globe is something Mercator's map lost, had to give up, to lie flat.

Even more of this "connectedness" is lost when we cut the sphere up into twelve gores. On *interrupted* maps like these, space—blank paper—seems to get between one part of the world and another. Goode's homolosine, above, is a familiar interrupted projection. Most projections preserve a sense of connectedness, but only by giving up something else.

Every Projection Has To Give Up Something To Get the Attributes It Has

For example, we saw in the last chapter that in order to show "true" areas, Peters had to sacrifice—give up—"true" form. This had nothing to do with any inadequacy of his projection. It is simply that both of

these characteristics cannot be shown on a plane at the same time. This mutual exclusivity is, as it were, the form the "wrinkling" takes.

No map can show both true areas and true shapes.

Professional mapmakers call the ability to show true areas *equivalence*, and they call projections with this ability **equivalent**.

They call the ability to show true shapes *conformality*, and projections with this ability **conformal**.

In this language of mapmakers, no projection (and so no map) can be both equivalent *and* conformal.

We saw how terribly the *conformal* (true shape) Mercator distorts sizes. On the Mercator, Africa and Greenland look about the same size, but Africa is actually 14 times larger than Greenland.

On the other hand, we saw how the *equivalent* (true size) Peters distorts shapes: one mapmaker has said it makes the continents look like "wet, ragged long winter underwear hung out to dry on the Arctic Circle," and that it makes the world appear as "in a fun-house mirror."

Other projections show true distances, at least from selected points or lines, as we shall see in the next chapter. Professional mapmakers call these **equidistant**.

> **CONFORMAL:** Maps that present the shapes of things as they are on the globe.
>
> **EQUIVALENT or EQUAL-AREA:** Maps that display areas in their true proportions.
>
> **EQUIDISTANT:** On equidistant maps distance is shown accurately from a selected point or line.

Professional mapmakers call projections that show true directions *azimuthal*.

No single projection, and so no map, can display all these characteristics at the same time.

It is all about choosing the projection that serves our purpose.

> **AZIMUTHAL (ăz'ə·mŭth'əl):** "azimuth" means "bearing" or "direction." On azimuthal maps the directions from the point in the center to every other point are true.

Projections Are Like Points of View

For all these reasons different projections really are like points of view. If you are looking at a scene from over there, you cannot see it from over here. If you are admiring the appearance of the car in front of your house, you cannot be underneath it examining the exhaust system.

Each view excludes another. Because each view has its own value, each may be required to serve one purpose or another. But the more points of view that are taken into account, the more comprehensive is the understanding. This is especially true as we try to gain an understanding of the planet we live on.

We may imagine that once we have seen a picture of the earth from outer space, like the famous one of the earth rising over the moon, we have seen the planet as it really is (see page 72).

Nothing could be further from the truth. This image holds no more than we can see with our eyes. *There is so much more to the earth than this.*

For example, a recent issue of *Scientific American* magazine contained world maps showing the spread of early humans, changes in the risk of getting malaria, various temperatures on the surface of the sea, and where diseases broke out during the last El Niño.

None of these things can be seen with the eye, yet each contributes to our understanding of the earth. In collecting and analyzing the data and in setting them out for display, many different projections were used.

The Projection Is Not the Map

It is important to differentiate between a projection and its application in a particular map.

Attacks against "the Mercator," for example, are often wildly misplaced. People denigrate the Mercator projection as being out-of-date, obsolete, distorted, and an archaic holdover from our imperialist/colonialist past. We've even heard the Mercator decried as racist. The projection itself is *none* of these things. The objection *should* be directed against the projection's *misuse* as a world map when it was originally intended for the purpose of navigation. When the Mercator projection is misused it is not the projection that is at fault. Blame the mapmaker! Or the user!

A world map in the Mercator projection is *not*, as we have been describing it to this point, a "Mercator map." Such a map is simply (to repeat) *a world map in the Mercator projection*. Indeed, as we have just seen in the *Scientific American* examples, not even "world map" is specific enough. When "the Mercator" is being criticized, most of the time the target is a "political map of the world in the Mercator projection."

We do not wish to beat this point to death, but it is *purpose* alone that determines the worth of a map.

We can think of no purpose that is served by projecting the world in Mercator's projection. There may be a purpose we are overlooking, but until we learn of it our statement stands. You may recall that even Mercator's own 1569 map was too small for navigation, that the projection was intended to be used on *regional* sea charts. In fact, the Mercator is a perfect choice for mapping small parts of the globe. As a projection for world maps, however, the Mercator does not have much utility. It has more disadvantages than strengths.

When the great *utility* of Mercator's projection both for navigation and the mapping of small regions is taken into account, along with its lamentable *application* in world maps, especially world political maps, the importance of distinguishing the projection from the map should be very clear.

The Peters provides another example of this distinction. The Peters projection has sometimes been called the Gall-Peters projection. This is in tribute to James Gall who in 1885 was the first to publish this cylindrical equal-area projection.

Gall was motivated, as others had been, by a desire for a world map free of the Mercator's size distortions. Gall recognized that what he called his "orthographic" projection distorted shapes. He felt that the advantages of showing true areas outweighed this drawback.

And Gall was not the first to create a cylindrical equal-area projection. In 1772, J.H. Lambert, a German physicist, astronomer, mathematician and philosopher, published seven original map projections. Among these was the first cylindrical equal-area projection. (Included among the others was the Lambert conformal conic we mentioned in Chapter 1.)

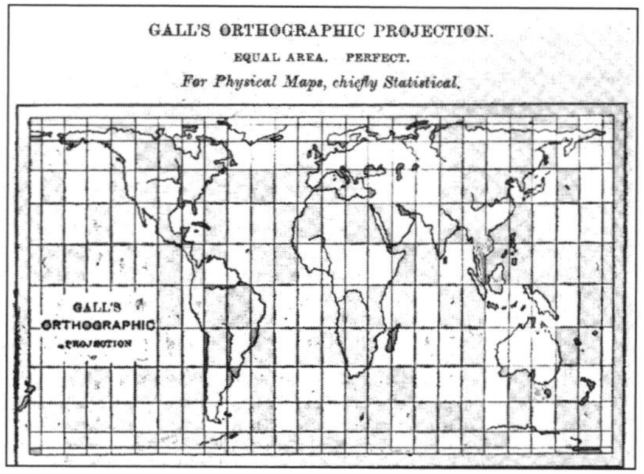

23

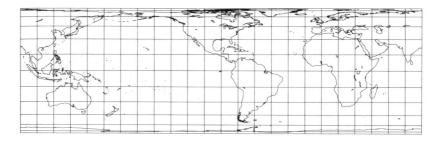

Figure 16. *This is a modern version of the simplest equal-area projection of the earth. The brilliant mathematician J.H. Lambert created this map in 1772. The extreme compression toward the poles makes it awkward for world maps, and he did not recommend it for such a purpose.*

You can see the family resemblance among these projections. All three have grids with straight lines that cross each other at right angles, as well as marked elongation of places toward the poles (look at what happens to Alaska for instance).

GALL'S ORTHOGRAPHIC PROJECTION.

EQUAL AREA.   PERFECT.

For Physical Maps, chiefly Statistical.

GALL'S ORTHOGRAPHIC PROJECTION

Figure 15. *This is Gall's Orthographic Projection of 1885. It is an equal-area projection. Gall was a clergyman motivated to find a projection without the exaggeration of the Mercator. He recognized that his projection distorted shapes but felt the trade-off was worth it.*

24

Like Gall and Peters, Lambert was especially pleased with how well the tropics showed up in his equal-area projection. In fact, Lambert illustrated the utility of his projection by showing how well it displayed Africa (see Fig. 17).

Figure 17. *Lambert's equal-area projection had no distortion at all along the equator. Because of this it was ideal for mapping the equatorial region. This is Lambert's own 1772 map of Africa.*

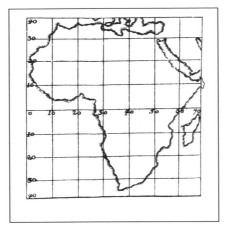

Lambert's equal-area projection never caught on for maps of the whole world because of its extreme distortion in the polar regions.

Gall's version reduced the distortion of the poleward regions, but even so his projection did not catch on. Walter Behrmann derived another version in 1910, and Trystan Edwards came up with still another in 1953. In 1974 Arno Peters published his version, almost identical to Gall's.

Peters, however, was more convincing when he argued that his projection's ability to show true areas *outweighed* its distortions of shape.

Peters' timing was good, too. By the 1970s people had become more sensitive to the role of perception in shaping attitudes and beliefs. In the post-colonial world then emerging, people were more interested in envisioning a world—and therefore a world map—that

gave all areas their fair share of the space. Equatorial regions, given short-shrift by the prevailing popular projections (Mercator foremost among them), were represented in an area-accurate manner on the Peters. In the public mind (or eye) equatorial countries were seen by many for the first time as really huge. Or, as some might say, showing the world in true proportion put the temperate latitudes, like the USA and Europe, "in their place."

This change in attitude played a big part in the acceptance of the Peters, for as we have seen it was anything but new.

Indeed non-cylindrical equal-area projections predated even Lambert's work. The sinusoidal projection, often called the Sanson-Flamstead, is an equal-area projection that dates to 1570. When this projection is used for maps of the world it has what some feel is an awkward shape (Refer to Figure 18-A to your right).

On the other hand, people may like the shape of the Mollweide. Karl Mollweide announced his equal-area projection in 1805. Like many other equal-area projections it is shown in an ellipse (see Figure 18-B).

This is also true of the equal-area projection Ernest Hammer introduced in 1892 (see Figure 18-C).

Max Eckert published three popular equal-area projections in 1906. Two are shown in Figure 18 (D & E).

The Boggs eumorphic projection, introduced in 1929, is another equal-area projection. It is usually seen as here, in Figure 18-F, in its interrupted form, like the Goode's homolosine we illustrated earlier. The Goode's, which is also equal area, fuses the sinusoidal and the Mollweide (Figures 18-A & 18-B).

A B C

D E F

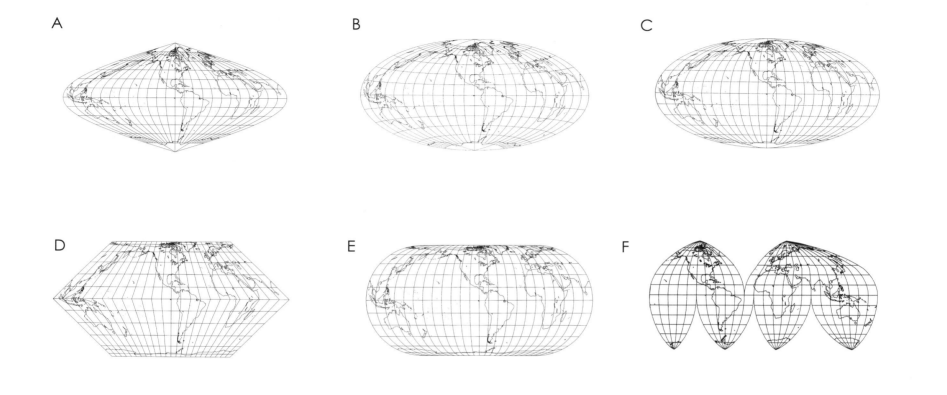

Figure 18. *Here are six further equal-area projections. From top left: (A) sinusoidal, (B) Mollweide, and (C) Hammer. From bottom left: (D) Eckert II, (E) Eckert IV and (F) Boggs eumorphic. There are still other ways of showing the world that are equal-area but differ in shape and the form of graticule. Which serves your interests best?*

These projections are but a few of the *many* equal-area projections mapmakers have developed. Some are rectangular. Some take the form of an ellipse. Some, like the sinusoidal or the Eckert II, have more unusual shapes. Depending on the shape, the parallels and the meridians may be straight or may be curved in differ-ent ways. Some of these projections are continuous; others are interrupted. Each shows true areas; each distorts shapes differently.

The choice among these projections depends on the purpose the map is intended to serve.

This View or That? An Average? Or Both?

As we have said, each projection amounts to a point of view. From over here you can see this. From over there you can see that. There is no place you can stand and see everything.

What about standing in between? Standing in between lets you see some of this and some of that. Mapmakers have taken such an "in-between" perspective by developing "compromise" or "arbitrary" projections. These are neither equal-area nor conformal but some of both. They are *more or less* conformal and *more or less* equal-area.

These have been widely used, for example, by the National Geographic Society in its maps of the world. The Society currently uses a compromise projection called the Winkel Tripel. From 1988 to 1998 it used a projection developed by Arthur Robinson. From 1922 to 1988, however, the Society used the Van der Grinten projection. About the Van der Grinten the Society once said, "In not attempting to show any special truth it gives perhaps the best over-all picture."

Certainly that is one way of thinking about it, but if you are standing in between you get *neither* full view, true shape *nor* true size. (We will look more closely at all these National Geographic projections in Chapter 4.)

What is wrong with *moving* from one view to another? First you catch this view. Then you get that. You stand in between for a while. Then you move to an entirely new position.

In fact, this is our recommendation. We believe that the best understanding comes from being able to view the world from as many perspectives as possible. We want you to give up the idea that one map, or even one projection, can meet our needs for understanding.

We want you to accept that different things can be seen from different points of view and to take as many points of view as possible. This acknowledges not only that different things can be seen from different perspectives, but that the world exceeds any single point of view. To see the world at all means to see it from many perspectives.

It is useful to be familiar with many different kinds of projections, each with its own slant. It is like getting to know a poem in a language you do not understand. Each new translation reveals a facet the other translations ignored. The more translations you read, the surer your "triangulation" on the poem you are trying to get to know.

The best way to understand our world is to view it through as many lenses as possible, to see it from as many vantage points as we can.

One projection is not in itself better than another.

Though one projection may be more appropriate than another for a specific use or purpose, each takes its own perspective, each makes its own translation of the globe.

The equal-area Peters is often contrasted to the constant compass-bearing Mercator because they are so glaringly different. We *appreciate* this contrast because it shocks viewers into questioning their assumptions about maps in particular and life in general. It helps people to "think outside the box" by exploring how what they see is predicated on what they expect to see.

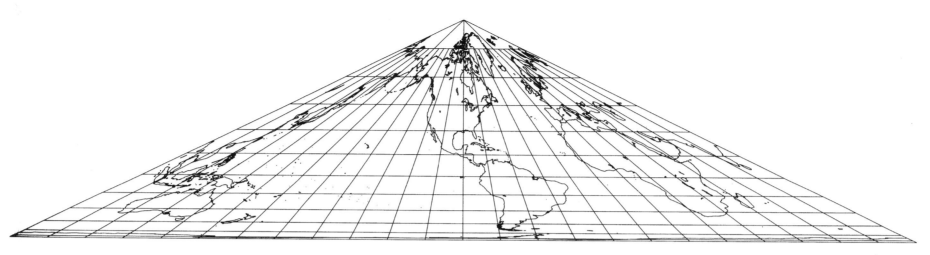

Figure 19. *Here's a rectilinear equal-area projection which manages to show one of the poles as the point it is!
You would want to use this projection for squeezing an equal-area map into a triangular shoulder patch.
Just one more point of view!*

Questions

Q: I heard someone say that the Mercator projection is racist, or that it is a white male conspiracy. Is there any truth to that?

A: That kind of talk is uninformed and has little merit. A projection is not racist. A projection may be used—inappropriately—because it represents the self-interests of a group—in this case privileged, mainly white, European or North American commercial interests. North Americans and Europeans HAVE grown accustomed to and are enamored of the self-importance the Mercator engenders (those countries do look more important on that projection). But the Mercator projection was created for NAVIGATION, and for that purpose it is still a superior tool. It is not that you SHOULDN'T have a Mercator in your classroom, it is that you probably would want to have other points of view as well. In fact, one of the most important skills any of us can acquire is to learn how to look at things from a VARIETY of points of view.

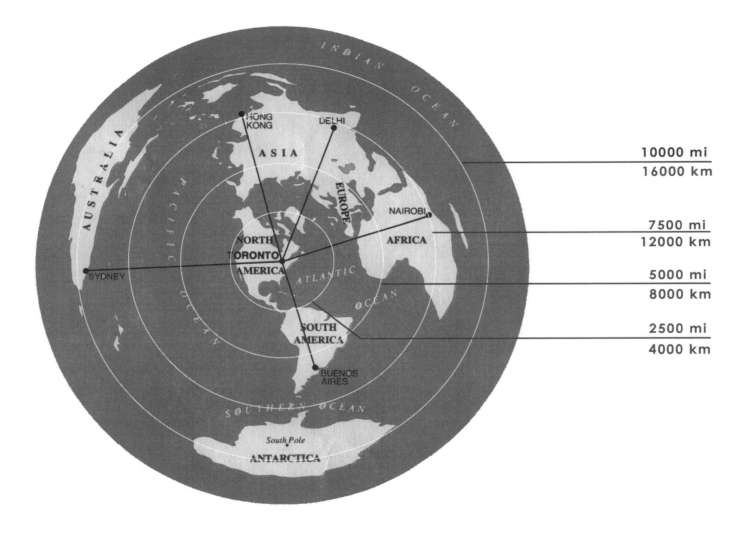

Figure 20. *Does the world revolve around Toronto, as this map seems to show?*

Every Map Comes In a Package

You get a new gadget—a sound system, a scooter, a food mixer, whatever—and your first priority is to open it up. Until you unpack it, the item is useless, even in your way.

It's like that with maps. As we have seen, every map comes packaged with a purpose. That purpose determines which properties the map needs to have, whether it needs to show true relative sizes or shapes, directions or distances. It is these *properties*, these *characteristics,* that make the map what it is, that enable the map to achieve its purpose.

It is time to get down to some serious unpacking. We will do this by actually viewing and assessing a variety of maps. Each map we have chosen is valuable and interesting in itself, but each will also serve as an entry point into certain map-making rules and realities that you'll be able to carry with you. It will be most effective if you participate in the process and take the time to complete the excercises in this book.

It's Your World, Toronto

Does the world revolve around Toronto, as the map to the left seems to show?

Look at this map. Take a second look, a good look. What do you think of it? Would you call this is an accurate map of the world? If you think it is, why? If you do not, why not?

If you recognize North and South America, do you also recognize Africa? How about Australia? Let's get really specific: trace Australia's shape onto a separate sheet of paper. Leave the name off. Show it to some friends—how many people looking at this do you suppose are going to say, "Of course that's Australia—anybody would recognize it"?

Why would an honest mapmaker—in this case, Leonard Guelke—make a map that distorts some land masses so severely?

Now note another feature of the map. The circles marked 2500 miles, 5000 miles and so on, all center on Toronto. Draw a straight line on this map from Toronto to anywhere in the world and, with some simple math, you've got the real-world distance.

This map uses an azimuthal equidistant projection. This particular example sets Toronto at the center, but a good mapmaker could prepare a map like this centered wherever you choose—on your town, on your favorite ski resort, on the North Pole.

EQUIDISTANT: On equidistant maps distance is shown accurately from a selected point.

AZIMUTHAL: "Azimuth" means "bearing" or "direction." Thus, an azimuthal map shows true directions.

Neat? Sure. Useful? Of course. But as we know, to show one truth you have distort another. On any map of the world "something has got to give." A world map that correctly shows distances from a central point *must* sacrifice other qualities.

Which? Accuracy of some shapes, as we have just demonstrated with the tracing of Australia. Precise sizes for another. Compare Australia and North America: which looks larger? In spite of what this map seems to tell us, Australia is really less than a third of the size of North America.

This map has limitations even with regard to distance. You can accurately measure the distance from Toronto to, say, Paris, France or to Caracas, Venezuela, but not between Caracas and Paris. The given scale does not apply. The only constant distances are those from Toronto. That's what the map claims. That's exactly what it delivers.

Is this a good map? Actually, it is a very good map—for a very limited purpose. But as soon as you try to make it do something it was not intended to do, you

have created a problem. Note the language: the map doesn't create the problem, the user does.

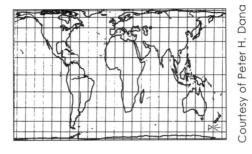

Courtesy of Peter H. Dana

Figure 21. *Is this really how you expect the world to look on a map?*

The Peters Map of the World

We first showed you the Peters map in Chapter One, and we also discussed it in Chapter Two. You know what we said about it, but what do *you* think? Does it strike you as an accurate, reliable image of the world? If you answer "yes," can you give reasons for your answer? If you say "no," on what factual basis have you made up your mind?

Thinking aside, how does it make you feel? Some who have looked at it for the first time, or even after many times, talk of feeling angry, puzzled, inquisitive, surprised—even amused.

Unlike Guelke's map centered on Toronto, the Peters world map lays no claim to accuracy of distance. It makes a very different claim: to present the relative size of areas with complete accuracy.

As we know, this means the Peters takes its place among equal-area or equivalent projections.

As with Guelke's equidistant map, so with the Peters: "something has got to give," something must be sacrificed. What would you say it is? We have already agreed that the shapes of continents you are familiar with have been compromised, but how serious is this problem for you? Are the shapes of the major land masses twisted beyond recognition, or do you still recognize them without difficulty? How different are they from true shapes on a globe?

Some land areas appear to be stretched vertically; others, horizontally. To be more precise, this projection uses two "base" or "standard" lines, here 45° N and 45° S. These are approximately the lines running through Portland, Oregon (or Milan, Italy) and through New Zealand's South Island (or the Archipelago de los Chonos, Chile). Along these two lines, and only along these two lines, is the map's given scale constant. Between these lines—which of course are parallels of latitude—shapes are pulled in a north-south direction; beyond them they are stretched east-west.

Why? Just one reason: in order to accomplish the map's clear goal, which is to represent the sizes of all areas with complete accuracy.

Do you recognize the principle that is emerging? One way to state it might be: every map has its purpose. *Only when you have unpacked that purpose are you ready to judge the map itself.* You've got to "see through" the opaqueness of the printed map to the mapmaker's intention. Always judge a map by its central aim, not by some extraneous standard. Remember that, judged by the purpose for which it was intended, the Duke guard's sketch map was perfect.

Which does not mean that either the guard's sketch or the Peters is perfect for every need.

To restate the point more generally: everything is for something. A shovel is great for digging in the ground; a spoon is useful for eating soup. The important thing is never to confuse them.

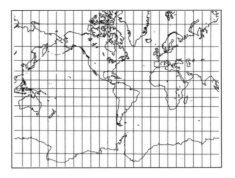

Figure 22. *Familiar? From the days of sailing ships and European colonization comes this image of the world.*

The Mercator

We know you have seen this map before, because we spent a lot of time in Chapter One and a bit in Chapter Two talking about Mercator, his projection and world maps that use it.

Many people claim this is the best known map of the world, seen more often, by more people, than any other. Newspapers and news magazines regularly use it. Classrooms—elementary schools, middle schools, high schools, even colleges—may have Mercator maps hanging on their walls. TV stations often display it as a backdrop for world news reports. You may even have seen it when the United States Secretary of State was interpreting foreign policy.

The Mercator image of the world is used commercially to help sell clocks, computer software, travel and management services. Even some global-minded humanitarian agencies display it. The manager of a prominent map store in New York City readily admits that he sells more Mercator wall maps than those of any other projection. He is not happy about it, but he recognizes demand where it exists.

34

Why might he not be happy about this state of affairs? One reason might be that the Mercator projection has two sterling attributes that make it a poor choice for mapping the world:

1) As we saw in Chapter One, straight lines drawn on a Mercator are lines of constant compass bearing. This is a useful property for sailing and air travel, but in either case *a world map is too small* for useful navigation. For use in navigation, the Mercator is more useful in larger, *regional* charts.

2) As we also saw in Chapter One, the Mercator is conformal, that is, it portrays shapes accurately. But as we also saw, it does this only locally. (Recall the different shapes of the head drawn on the four different projections.) For this reason too the Mercator is a great choice for mapping small areas.

Both strengths of the Mercator are best exploited in maps of small areas: in sailing or flying charts, or in very large-scale (that is, relatively small area) topographical mapping. On a world map these strengths turn into horrible weaknesses because they are achieved at the cost of a terrible distortion of sizes.

People who know maps shudder whenever they see the Mercator projection used as a "general purpose" map of the world. As early as 1918 Gilbert Grosvenor, president of the National Geographic Society, called it "atrocious." More recently Arthur Robinson, a mapmaker we will get to know better in the next chapter, has asserted that, as a picture of the world, the Mercator map "is just awful."

Yet these and other experts have been unable to wean people from the Mercator image.

Just why *is* the Mercator so popular?

Largely it is popular because it *was* popular. It was popular because in the colonial ages of sail and steam the technical practicality of the Mercator *projection* gave the *projection* immense authority.

If Europe's educated landspeople were not in a position to use the actual Mercator sailing charts, they clearly benefitted from colonial trade and European naval might, which did utilize Mercator charts. And they could hang Mercator maps of the world in their parlors and their children's classrooms. For most of the 18th and all of the 19th centuries the Mercator was accepted as *the* map of the world, mostly because the *projection* was so essential to the sailor, explorer, whaler, and navy navigator. The prestige the map had among Europeans gave it an even greater prestige among colonial peoples who often opted to imitate their colonial masters.

This is a good example of the perils we talked about in Chapter Two of confusing the projection with the map. While the projection was eminently useful for preparing charts, its application to a widely disseminated world map was a terrible mistake.

Try This!

Take a pencil and on the next page, without looking at a map, draw a picture of the world. Many people find this intimidating but—go on—no one is watching! Let yourself go. Take whatever time you need to dredge up from your memory the necessary details.

Keep an eraser handy. As you work you may realize how much more you know than you thought you knew, and you are going to want to rework some first efforts.

Figure 23.

MY VIEW OF THE WORLD

TODAY'S DATE _____

36

Of course you have a double advantage in this exercise. You are in that special category of people who enjoy, or are at least challenged by, geography. (Why else would you be reading this book?) And having gotten this far into the book, you have fresh images of the world in your memory bank.

We have conducted experiments like this many times. So have others. After you finish your sketch you may want to take another look at the map made by the Duke student, Mark Fisher, which we reproduced in Chapter Two (page 17). Also compare your result with the two examples on this page. One is by Andrew Kent, a middle school student in California. Andrew has had the advantage of considerable travel—over much of the United States and Canada and overseas, which probably helped him as he drew. The other was done by Jessica Kim, in a Gifted and Talented program in her New Jersey high school. Both maps were done from memory, just as yours has been.

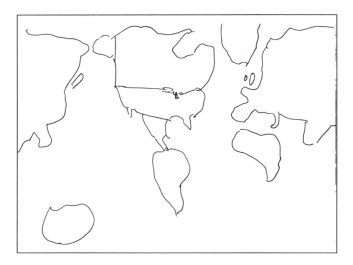

Figure 25. *The world according to Jessica Kim.*

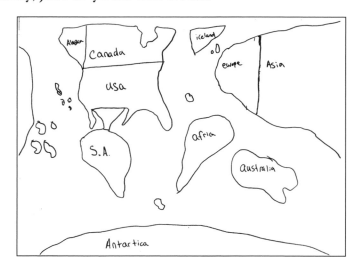

Figure 24. *The world according to Andrew Kent.*

Thomas Saarinen supervised the collection of maps like these from students at 75 universities in 52 countries. He has analyzed 3,568 hand-drawn maps of the world. The results are clear:

- We all have maps of the world "in our heads" that we can turn into sketches.
- More often than not we center the map around the region we live in.
- We know our own region best, and fill it in with the most detail.
- These "mental maps" tend to exaggerate the northern hemisphere while downplaying areas near, and south of, the equator. Europe, Greenland and Canada are regularly shown larger than they really are. Greenland is sometimes blown up to about 600 times its actual size.
- Even people who do not live in Europe or North America tend to exaggerate the prominence of those areas, mimicking the lopsidedness of Mercator-based maps.

Given these results, can there can be any doubt that the Mercator image of the world remains very influential? As an image, it powerfully shapes the worldview of countless people.

If your drawing does not fall into the "Mercator-in-the-mind" trap, congratulations! You have already begun your journey to a better informed, more realistic understanding of the world and of the maps that portray it.

Spaceship Earth: Buckminster Fuller's Dymaxion World

This striking map was invented by Buckminster Fuller in 1927. Fuller has been variously described as an architect, inventor, designer, environmentalist, mathematician, educator, poet, philosopher, genius and socially conscious human.

Fuller's consuming interest was to help people develop a more rational, sustainable approach to living

FULLER PROJECTION

Figure 26. Don't throw it out until you've unpacked it!

38

on the earth. Because Fuller thought big—in global terms—he worked with world maps.

He became increasingly unhappy with what he saw as inappropriate uses of the Mercator. Fuller was particularly critical of publishers for continuing to offer Mercator maps for general use when they should have known better. In 1927 he created his own projection, though it only achieved notoriety sixteen years later when *Life* magazine published the map as a cutout in 1943.

The visionary Fuller saw a world in change, a world which "has called for a revolution in map making and in cartographical principles such as history has never seen." Certainly his map shakes people out of their world-map rut, but does it satisfy the need for the revolution that Fuller saw?

What hits you as you look at this map? What do you see as its strengths? How about its shortcomings? Would you say it presents sizes and shapes well? Is it a map you could navigate by? Can you use it to judge distances? If you hung it on your wall, how would it help you relate more realistically to the world?

Would you agree with Fuller that it can help us recognize that "we're all astronauts aboard a little spaceship called Earth"?

Would you agree that Fuller accomplished another goal: "No longer need the American continents, for instance, with only twelve percent of the world population, occupy relentlessly the central and non-distorted portion of the world map, assigning fifty-two percent of the world's population to an insignificant, fragmented, and distorted Asiatic borderline position."

The Dymaxion World Map does show all land areas without significant distortion of size or shape. On the other hand, directions—and therefore spatial relationships—are unintelligible. As for distance, the map lays no claim to be distance-accurate.

Fuller's Dymaxion map has a number of strengths. But if you haven't decided to run to your nearest map store to get a few copies, you belong to a large club. In part because it seems strange to the eye and the brain, in part because of its broken surface and sharp angles, this map has never achieved a high level of acceptance among either professional cartographers or the general public.

Does this say something about the map? Or does it say something of our prejudices about the way a map of the world is supposed to look?

Five Questions To Ask About Any Map Projection

What we have begun here is a process of "unpacking" or "decoding" maps. Such a process requires us to equip ourselves with analytical tools—tools that will help us see through maps to discern their motivating agendas.

Without such tools we simply accept what maps tell us. Learning to ask the right questions can help to liberate our thinking. It can free us from bondage to other peoples' agendas. Why should we passively allow our minds to be taken over by someone else's image of the world?

Following are five questions you might want to ask yourself when you are looking at a map, especially when you are looking at a map of the world or a big piece of it.

Because every map is a trade-off between competing properties, the answers to these questions do not imply that a projection is good or bad. The questions merely aim to keep you sharp, attentive to the ways different projections create different images of reality.

1) Does the map show the world whole or does it break it up? In map talk the question is whether the world is displayed as continuous or interrupted.

Because every map has edges—which the spherical earth lacks—every map breaks the world up: every map "interrupts" the world at the map's edges. But some maps break up, or interrupt, the world to a marked degree. Fuller's Dymaxion World is a good example, but one of the world's most popular textbook maps, Goode's homolosine, is also significantly interrupted. We have already alluded to Goode's projection on page 21. In Chapter Five we look at it in detail.

2) What shape does the projection make the world?

Most of the examples we have shown you, like the Mercator and the Peters, set the world in a rectangular frame. But Guelke's Toronto-centered map turns the world into a circle, and Fuller's Dymaxion map renders it into a difficult-to-describe shape made up of triangles and squares (actually a flattened cuboctahedron). All interrupted maps, in fact, may be said to resist easy labelling. Toward the end of Chapter Two we presented projections that cast the world in a variety of ellipsoids and other shapes. The last map we showed in Chapter Two, Collignon's, even squeezed the earth into a triangle.

Each shape resulted from a desire to preserve or highlight some attribute of the earth: true sizes, for example, or distances. Or perhaps from a desire to make the projection as easy as possible to construct. Or just because no one had done it before.

There are, however, those who argue that some shapes are *inherently* preferable to others. In 1989 the preeminent association of professional mapmakers in the USA, the American Cartographic Association, urged publishers, broadcasters and governments to "Just Say NO" to rectangular maps with rectangular grids. Besides pointing out how

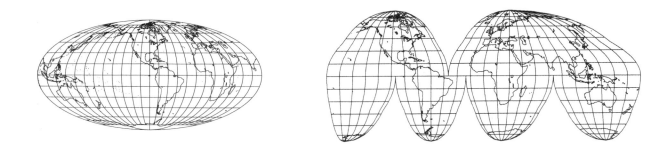

Figure 27. *On the Mollweide (left) the world appears smooth and whole. On the Goode (right) the world seems cut into sections. Which seems more realistic to you? Both are equal-area projections, but compare the portrayal of shapes. What does the Mollweide give up for the sense of continuity? What does the Goode gain by being interrupted?*

badly the most popular of these projections distort either size (the Mercator) or shape (the Peters), the mapmakers argue that these maps *visually betray the fact that the earth is round.*

Adherents of the Peters projection, on the other hand, insist that a simple rectangular grid is more "user-friendly." They feel the fact that meridians on the earth *do* converge at the poles is less important than helping users "get their bearings," with north-south and east-west lines predictably intersecting at right angles.

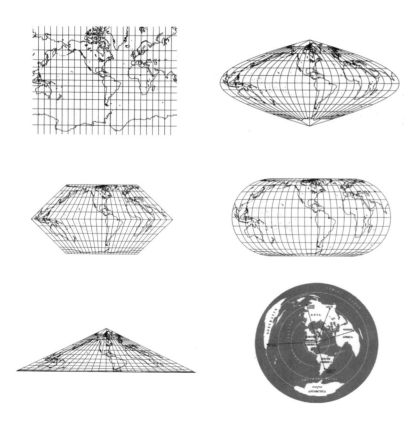

Figure 28. *Maps come in many shapes. Which suits you best?*

Can a flat map "betray" a spherical earth? Can straightening the earth's converging meridians help people better understand it? What do *you* think?

We do not want to make your decision for you, but we do want you to be fully alert to the question.

3) *How are the continents and oceans arranged?*

You are familiar with the usual arrangements: America on the left, Africa and Eurasia on the right with the Atlantic in the middle; or the Americas in the middle with Asia and the Pacific to the left and the Atlantic, Europe and Africa to the right.

It goes without saying that north is at the top.

Most of the world maps you have ever seen fall into one of these two camps. But not all of them. Guelke's map, centered on Toronto, presents a very different perspective.

Fuller's Dymaxion World puts Antarctica at the right. The Americas run across the middle of his map from right to left. Eurasia and Africa spread out at the left.

In the next chapter we will look at "upside-down" maps with south at the top. In these, the conventional view is flipped.

Is there a right way?

Again, every map is a point of view that lets you see *this*, but not *that*. If you want to see *that*, you need to take another point of view.

What do you think?

4) *Are the grid lines curved or straight?*

We touched on this in our discussion of the shape of the map, but the issues are not always related.

For example, the Van der Grinten, which we discuss in the next chapter, is enclosed in a circle. Usually, however, the polar regions are lopped off and the projection is presented in a rectangle. Unless you pay atten-

You've seen these words before when we talked about the graticule.

The **GRATICULE** is made up of parallels and meridians.

MERIDIANS: The lines that run from pole to pole. They converge at the poles and diverge as they move toward the equator.

PARALLELS: The lines that run parallel around the earth, intersecting the meridians at 90 degrees.

tion you may miss the fact that within its rectangular frame most of the parallels and meridians are arcs of circles.

The issue lies at the heart of the difference between globes and maps. Say you stayed on the 40th parallel and walked west around the world. Okay, you would have to be able to walk on water, but let us say you can.

Although you would follow a straight line—undeviatingly—sooner or later you would end up where you started. That is, your straight line would simultaneously be a circle.

This is just the way things are on a globe.

On a Mercator or Peters your walk would show up as a *straight line* passing from one side of the map to the other.

On a map like Guelke's, but centered on one of the poles instead of Toronto, your walk would show up as a *perfect circle*.

Which is right? Which is better?

Does it not depend on what you want the map for? What do you think?

5) Do the parallels and meridians cross at right, or at larger or smaller, angles?

On the globe parallels and meridians cross at right angles everywhere. Yet at the same time the meridians converge toward the poles.

This can happen on a sphere. It cannot happen on a plane.

That is, on the globe the parallels—the lines of latitude—are getting shorter and shorter toward the poles; and this means that the areas they enclose are getting smaller and smaller too. A quadrilateral bounded by two parallels and two meridians close to one of the poles can be less than 1/25th the size of one near the equator.

Armed with this information, look at a map. Do the parallels and meridians cross at right angles? If they do, what is happening to the size of the areas they bound?

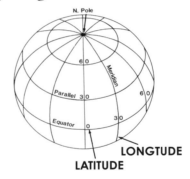

Figure 29. The graticule.

On the Mercator, since its parallels and meridians *do* cross at right angles, the quadrilaterals get *larger and larger* toward the poles. This is the source of the exaggeration in the size of Greenland. Notice how Antarctica would become infinitely huge, which is why it is impossible to fully display Antarctica on a Mercator projection.

By way of contrast, check out the sinusoidal (Figure 30). As you can see, some of the intersections of parallels and meridians make right angles, but the majority do not. On the other hand, the parallels *do* get shorter, and so the meridians converge toward the poles as they do on the earth. Therefore the quadrilaterals get smaller just as they do on the earth.

In fact, they get smaller in the same proportion as those on the globe. As you may infer from this, the sinusoidal is equal-area. On the other hand, since the angles are not 90°, shape is distorted.

Which do you prefer? Again, doesn't it depend on what you are trying to understand?

It is not a matter of right and wrong. Every projection resolves the conflict between sphere and plane its own way. All we want to do is give you something to hang on to when you are wrestling with a map.

There are many more questions you can ask yourself as you think about the relationship between a map in your hands and the world it is claiming to represent. The five we have just asked are fundamental:

- Does the world look whole or broken up?
- What shape is given to the world (rectangular, circular, oval, other)?
- How are the land masses and oceans arranged?
- Are the grid lines straight or curved?
- Do the grid lines form right or other angles?

A summary of the answers to these questions for many of the projections and images in this book is found in Appendix B

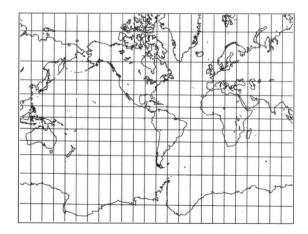
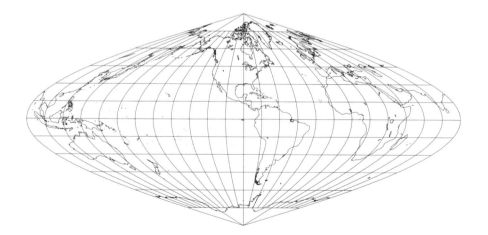

Figure 30. *The Mercator and sinusoidal projections.*

What are some other questions that occur to you?

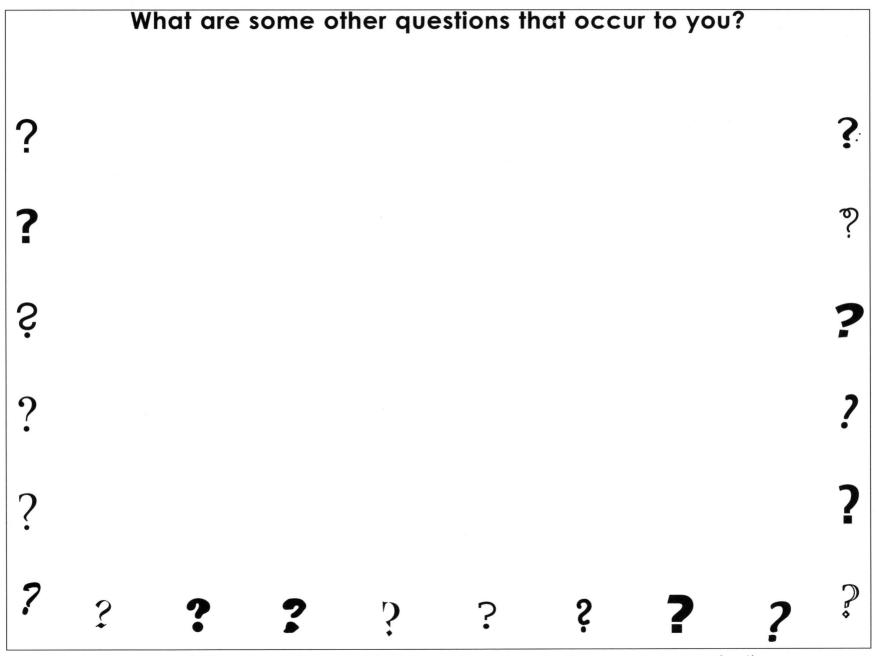

See page 124 for Bob Abramms' list of questions to ask about any map projection

Questions

Q: I'm starting to get the idea that there are more ways of making a map than I ever imagined. Is that part of what you're saying here?

A: Exactly! And every method, approach or projection has its own particular bias (or favorite things to emphasize). There is not necessarily a wrong or right, just a whole bunch of different views of the world!

Compromise Projections

Few people like to hear "No!"

So when they are told there is no way to show everything on a flat sheet of paper the way it is on the globe, they resist. Again and again people have struggled with this fact of nature.

Mathematicians, physicists, clergymen, astronomers, mapmakers, inventors, historians and others have turned their hands to the problem of map-making with varying results. In this way they have invented the enormous number of projections we know today.

There is no intrinsic limit to the number of projections that are possible. Several hundred have already been published. Thousands of others have been created but not widely circulated. These amount to a multitude of different perceptions of the globe!

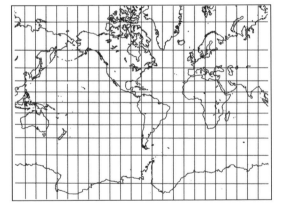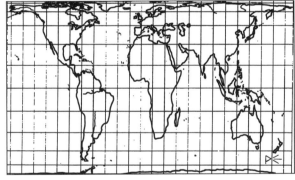

Figure 31. *Mercator was motivated by the utility for sailors of straight compass bearings. Peters was motivated by correcting the impression of the world created by a diet of too much Mercator. Other mapmakers have had other motivations.*

46

You are more likely to see some of these projections than others. In the last chapter we commented on the prevalence of the image of the world brought into being by Mercator's projection. In fact, it is precisely the shortcomings of this image that have prompted many of the new projections. A prime example of this is the family of equal-area projections inaugurated by Lambert in 1772, which led through Gall to Peters and his projection of 1974.

But there are very many others, prompted by considerations other than those that motivated Mercator or Peters.

As we have seen, maps that preserve shapes cannot show the areas of places as they are on the globe. On the other hand, maps that are equal-area cannot show shapes the way they are on the globe. Most inventors of map projections have tried to reduce these consequences, or to limit them to regions they consider of lesser importance. Often these are the polar regions.

Such compromise projections are among the most common in the world today. Those that get adopted by the major publishers of maps are seen by many, many millions of people.

One of the most important, and most influential, publishers of maps is the National Geographic Society. Millions of their maps find their way into schools and the homes of Society members around the world several times a year. Whether users realize it or not, the projections selected by the Society for its world maps have entered deeply into the consciousness of our times.

Today the Society uses a compromise projection called the Winkel Tripel. Earlier, from 1988 to 1998, the Society used a projection developed by Arthur Robinson.

From 1922 to 1988, however, the Society used the Van der Grinten projection. In this chapter we will be looking at each of these projections in turn, all of which are widely used by other publishers as well as the National Geographic Society. In fact, we will make our approach to the Van der Grinten by looking at a map of the world which takes a very unusual point of view.

Figure 32. *These are the three projections the National Geographic Society has used for its world maps since 1922. On this page: the Van der Grinten*

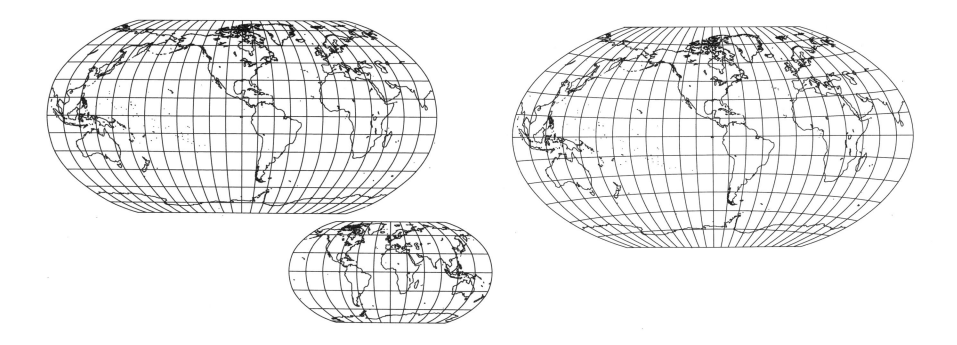

On this page, on the left are two Robinsons: the larger Americas-centered, below it an Africa-centered version. To the right is the Winkel Tripel. How much difference do you discern in the treatment of the continents on these three projections?

48

An Upside Down Map

When some people see the map on page 49 for the first time their impulse is to turn it over. That is, they want to hold the map so that North America is on their left and Asia is on their right the way they usually hold the map when the Atlantic is in the middle. Of course they soon realize that held this way the type is upside down and that they are looking at an upside down map of the world.

So they turn it right side up, that is, so that Asia is on their left and North America is on their right and the type can be read. This map is right side up only when it appears upside down.

It is confusing when you think about it. When you are finished thinking about it, everything is a little more sharply focused. That is why this map is so refreshing: though at first it befuddles, it ends up by clarifying.

It is a graphic example of what we mean by . . . thought provoking. This "What's Up? South!" map just happens to be published on a Van der Grinten projection. But it could have been produced on the Peters, the Mercator, or any other projection.

The thing is, we get into ruts so easily. By the time we leave school, even if we never graduated, we have seen so many maps of the world with north at the top—that we come to think this must be the way it is, the way the world is.

But it is merely the way we are used to seeing it. The world does not have a top. It is a ball and we can roll it anyway we want and look at it from any point of view. What we put on top is a matter of habit, of convention, of emphasis.

Another map which has us question, "Which way is up?" is seen on page 51. This *perspective* map, created by Russell Lenz, shows how the USA looks as seen from Canada. Things *seem* turned upside down, but they're not. It is just another point of view.

Historically, maps have been made with a variety of directions on top. The wall-sized map carved onto

Figure 33. *This is a fragment of a wall-size scale map of Rome from just after AD 200. It was carved in marble. It is oriented with southeast to the top.*

marble tablets in 3rd century Rome is oriented with southeast to the top. An early Medieval "Isidore" map is bound south up, though the writing is every which way so it does not really have a top at all. Often maps had an obvious natural feature at the top to make orientation easy. Swiss and other maps, for example, were

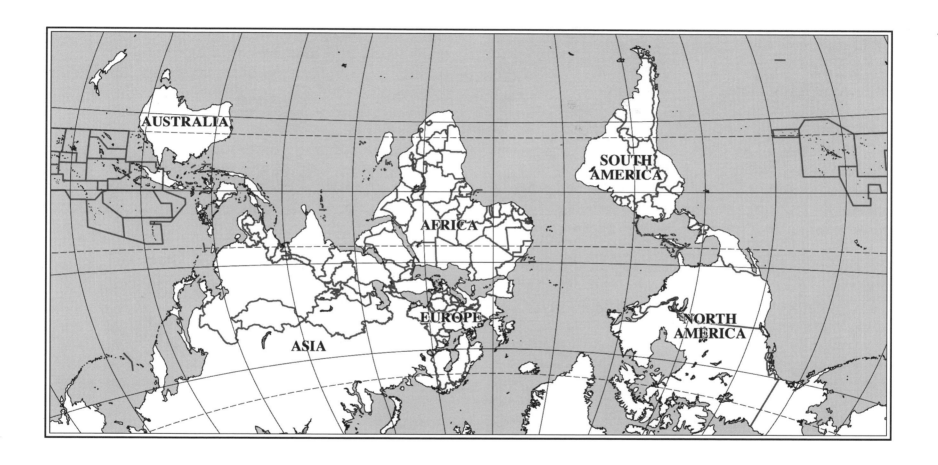

Figure 34. This is the "What's Up? South!" Map. It's just a map of the world. Our custom of putting north at the top is nothing but prejudice and habit.

50

long oriented to the south where the Alps made a natural horizon. Maps of north Italy were oriented to the north for the very same reason.

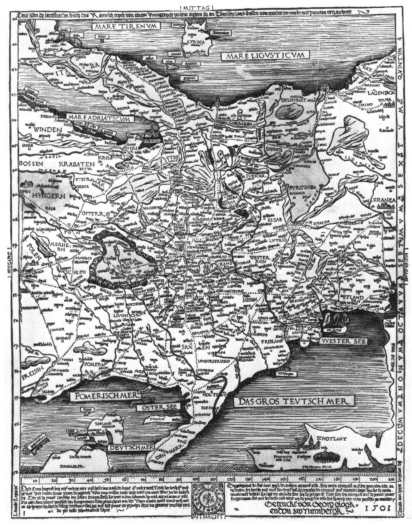

Figure 35. *Here's another map with south at the top, from 1501. It was made by Erhard Etzlaub, from Nuremberg, which lies near the center of the map. The 'boot' of Italy runs into the upper left-hand corner of the map.*

Most European world maps had east at the top until the sixteenth century. East was "the direction of Paradise." In fact our word "orientation" comes from *oriens*, the Latin word for "east". *Oriens* came from *oriri*, "to rise," and it came to refer to the east because that's where the sun "rises."

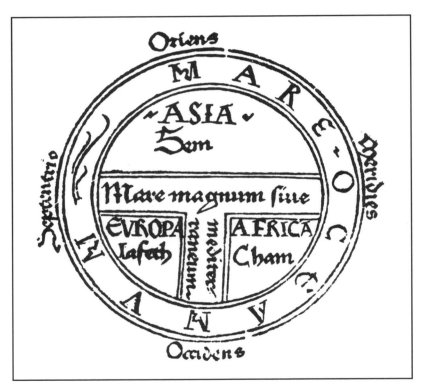

Figure 36. *An early European map of the world oriented with east at the top. Note the word 'Oriens,' or 'East,' above the encircling ocean. Note the 'T' inside a circle. That is why it is referred to as a 'T&O' map.*

The sun "rises" because the earth turns. It is this turning that gives us our four cardinal directions: east is the direction the sun "rises," west is the direction it "sets," and north and south are the directions at either

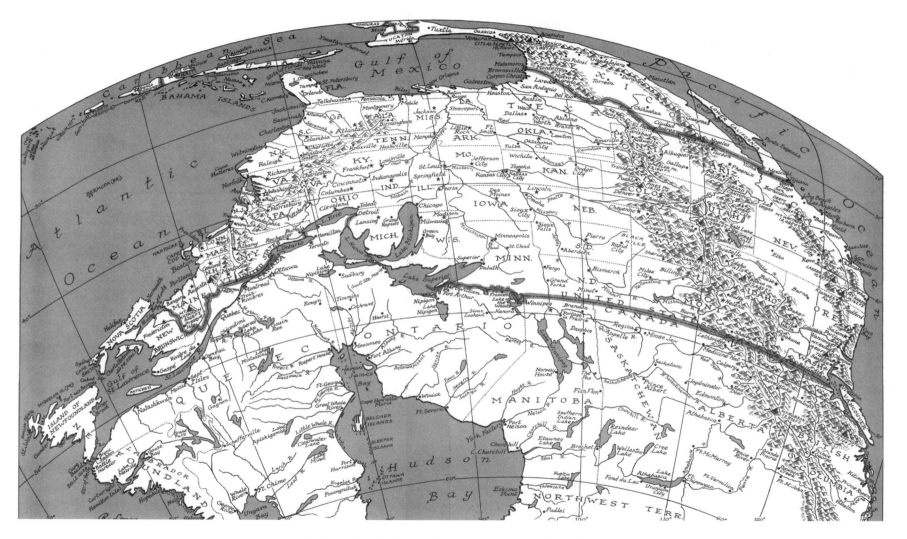

Figure 37. *The USA as seen from Canada*

end of the axis around which the planet spins. This spin also generates a magnetic field in which compass needles align themselves. Once people began using compasses, it began to make sense to orient maps to the compass, especially on the ocean where there were fewer natural features than on the land. Since compasses line up north-south, so did maps. Though there was a brief tradition of south-up maps oriented to south-pointing compasses—it is only convention after all that puts the arrow on one end or the other of a compass needle—world maps in particular began to follow the convention that north is up.

But north is not up. "Up" is over our heads, and when we mix "up" with "top" and "north" we do ourselves a disservice. We confuse all the other things we associate with "up" and "top" (like good and heaven) with north; and all the things we associate with "down" and "bottom" (like bad and hell) with south. So Australia is "down under" (under what?) and Antarctica is "the bottom of the world."

Look below: Antarctica does not even appear on the "What's Up? South!" map of the world.

Some world!

But then, as we know, it is hard to show the planet in its three-dimensioned sphericity on a two-dimensioned piece of paper.

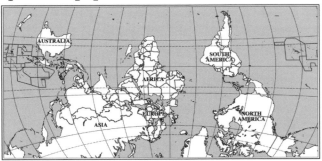

The Van der Grinten

Our "What's Up? South!" Map (Figure 34) is on the Van der Grinten projection. Alphons J. Van der Grinten invented the projection in 1898. In classifications of map projections it usually falls in the "other" category, which means it cannot easily be understood as the projection of the globe onto a cylinder, cone or plane. It is not equal-area or conformal either. It is a compromise projection, more or less equal-area and more or less conformal.

The National Geographic Society used the Van der Grinten for their world maps from 1922 to 1988. It is the map about which the Society made the claim we quoted earlier to the effect that, "In not attempting to show any special truth it gives perhaps the best overall picture."

This is a matter of opinion. Yet because the Van der Grinten does *sort of* preserve the shapes of things on the globe without the *huge* areal distortions of the Mercator, the projection has been one of the most popular in modern times. This was true in the Soviet realm as well as in the "West." The Van der Grinten was not only used for wall maps (second only to the Mercator), but in textbooks (where for years it ran second only to Goode's homolosine).

Many feel that its popularity reflects the historic prevalence of the Mercator; while the Van der Grinten does reduce the Mercator's areal distortion (though not all that much), it manages to look a lot like that very familiar map.

It manages to look like a Mercator despite the fact that its graticule is curved. Recall that meridians and parallels on the Mercator are straight lines that inter-

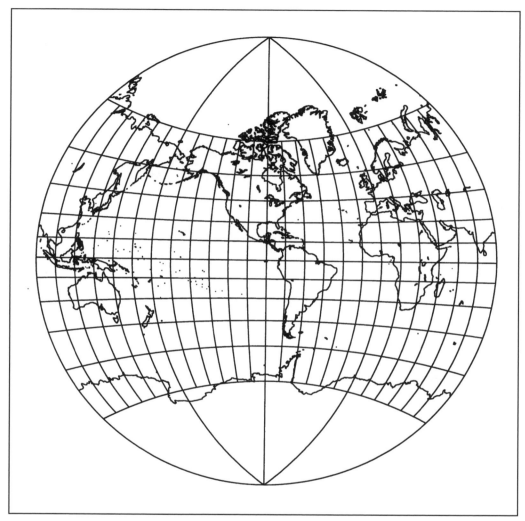

Figure 38. *The distortions of the continents look familiar to those accustomed to the Mercator on this projection invented by Alphons J. Van der Grinten in 1898. There was also something appealing about having the world in a circle.*

central meridian are straight lines. On our "What's Up? South!" map the central meridian is the Greenwich, or 0°, meridian. This intersects the equator at a right angle, 0° latitude and 0° longitude, near the center of the map. This happens to be in the Gulf of Guinea, just south of Ghana. On our "What's Up? South!" Van der Grinten projection map, south means toward the top.

All the rest of the meridians and parallels are arcs of circles, and none of them intersects anything at right angles. Furthermore, the meridians meet at the poles. This means that the Van der Grinten is enclosed in a circle. This was once seen as very attractive, but today the polar regions are usually lopped off and the projection presented in a rectangle, as in the "What's Up? South!" version on page 49.

With this map before us we can ask not only whether one projection is better than another, but whether a certain orientation is preferred. No, and again no! Though one may be more appropriate than another for a specific purpose, each takes its own perspective on, makes its own translation of the globe. While some might see this map as doubly distorted, we prefer to see it as doubly stimulating. Indeed, one of the most popular "upside down" maps, the one published by S. McArthur, carried the title, "McArthur's Universal Corrective Map of the World." In this way it explicitly challenged the "correctness" of the conventional point of view (See next page).

sect at right angles. Meridians and parallels on the Van der Grinten are straight lines and arcs of circles that rarely intersect at right angles. The equator and the

54

At last, the first move has been made—the first step in the long overdue crusade to elevate our glorious but neglected nation from the gloomy depths of anonymity in the world power struggle to its rightful position—towering over its northern neighbours, reigning splendidly at the helm of the universe.

Never again to suffer the perpetual onslaught of "downunder" jokes—implications from Northern nations that the height of a country's prestige is determined by its equivalent spatial location on a conventional map of the world.

This map, a subtle but definite first step, corrects the situation. No longer will the South wallow in a pit of insignificance, carrying the North on its shoulders for little or no recognition of her efforts. Finally, South emerges on top.

So spread the word. Spread the map!

South is superior. South dominates!

Long live AUSTRALIA—

RULER OF THE UNIVERSE!!

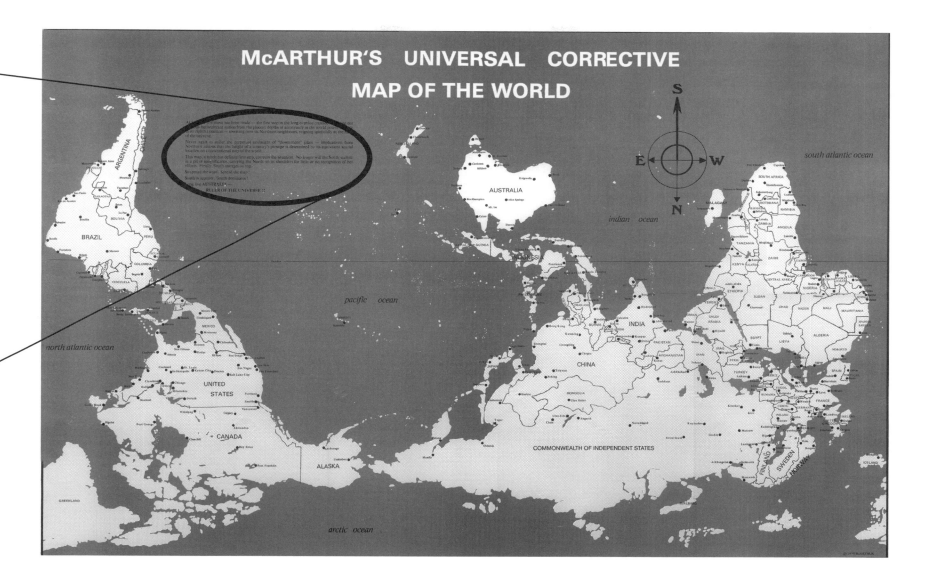

Figure 39. *Prejudices beg to be corrected. This is what* **McArthur's Universal Corrective Map of the World** *does to our prejudice about north being up.*

We appreciate this contrast because "upside down" maps shock viewers into questioning their assumptions about maps in particular and about life in general. As we said earlier about the contrast between the Mercator and the Peters, the contrast helps people to "think outside the box" by exploring how what they see is predicated on what they expect to see.

Sometimes all we need to do to solve our problems is turn them upside down.

Reactions
Learnings
New Insights

Figure 40. *This is Lambert's azimuthal equal-area projection. On this map with the north pole in its center, south is every direction from the center!*

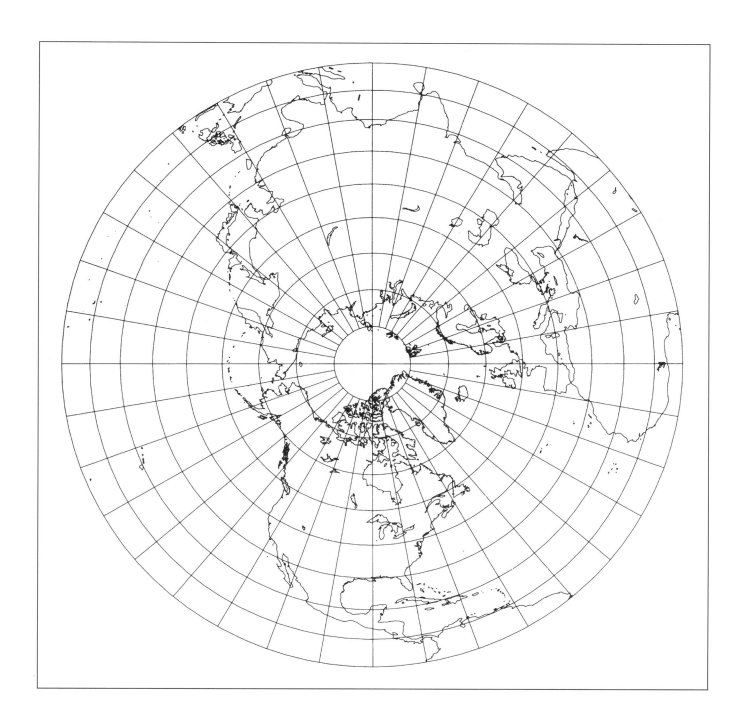

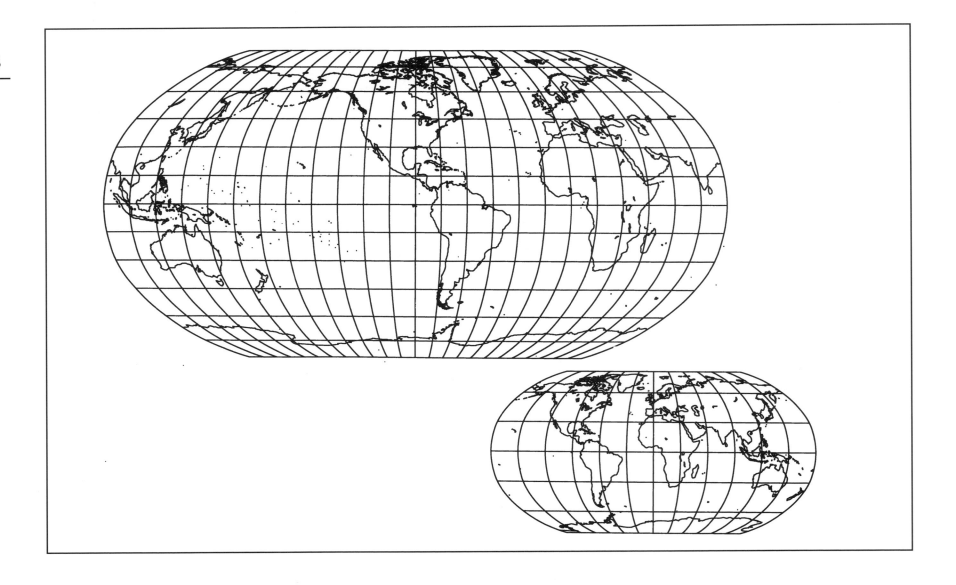

Figure 41. *The world as depicted by Arthur Robinson.*
The larger image shows the Americas in the center.
The smaller image simply re-centers the map on Africa.

Robinson Projection

You may well recognize this image (Figure 41). The projection was invented by Arthur Robinson in 1963, but it leapt into prominence in 1988 when the National Geographic Society adopted it in place of the Van der Grinten the Society had been using for the previous 66 years.

The National Geographic Society was enthusiastic about its new choice. "The trusty Van der Grinten was a good compromise. Arthur Robinson's projection is better still," the Society maintained.

But in what way was it better? The Society was forthright: whereas the Van der Grinten had shown Canada and the (former) Soviet Union at more than 200 percent of their actual size, the Robinson reduced this exaggeration to 150 percent.

What do *you* think about the projection?

Start with the size issue. Here it may be helpful to note the evolutionary development signified by how Greenland is shown. First, check the Mercator, where Greenland—a mere 0.8 million square miles—appears far larger than all of China with its 3.7 million square miles. The Van der Grinten trimmed Greenland slightly. The Robinson trimmed it even further, though its size remains distinctly exaggerated. (The Peters claims to have it right.)

There is no value in judging any of these maps by what they did not set out to do, but it is important to take seriously the National Geographic Society's claim that the Robinson is a better map than its predecessor because it exaggerates size less.

Given how much it continues to exaggerate the size of Greenland, do you think size was the Society's pri-mary consideration in adopting the Robinson, or were other factors at stake as well? We ask that you speculate on other possible reasons on the following page.

Next take the issue of shape. Compare the Robinson and Fuller's Dymaxion that we looked at in the last chapter. From the standpoint of what appear to you to be accurate renditions of shapes, how do the projections stack up?

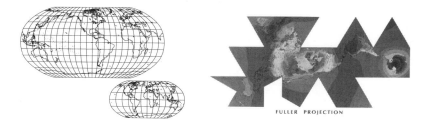

FULLER PROJECTION

To be sure this can be a tricky test: our mental image of "the right shape" may be less than totally reliable. Still, which of these two maps do you think is more nearly true? If you'd like to pursue the question of shape-fidelity further, compare both the Robinson and the Dymaxion with a good globe. A globe of even average quality will be more accurate than nearly any flat map.

Now think about directions. If you had the job of navigating across the open sea, would you prefer the Robinson or the Mercator?

To help yourself, pick two points, Lisbon, in Portugal, for example, and Recife, Brazil. Draw a straight line between them on both maps, then measure (or estimate if you don't have a protractor) the angles made by your line and the parallels and meridians it intersects. On the Mercator these angles are all the same. They vary on the Robinson.

REASONS THAT A PROFESSIONAL SOCIETY, TEACHER'S ASSOCIATION,
OR NATIONAL GOVERNMENT MIGHT WISH TO ALTER ITS
"OFFICIAL" PROJECTION:

Would it be easy to navigate with the Robinson?

If you were concerned about distances, would you be better off using an equidistant map (such as Guelke's Toronto-based map) or the Robinson? Don't jump to conclusions. Remember that equidistant projections show undistorted distances from selected points or lines only.

It is not that the Robinson fails these comparisons—each of the maps to which we compared the Robinson would fail at least three of them as well. Rather, the goal is to help you develop the skill of seeing through things—to start thinking freely and analytically about the claims adherents make for this or that projection.

Neither you nor we were among those who, on behalf of the National Geographic Society, made the decision to adopt the Robinson. Still, it may be worthwhile to imagine ourselves among them.

To do this it may be useful to review some of the claims Society officials have made over the years. Recall again what the Society said about the Van der Grinten, that, "In not attempting to show any special truth it gives perhaps the best over-all picture."

We have observed that this is a matter of opinion, but it is an opinion the Society has held to for most of its existence. Again and again the Society has avoided the alternatives offered by equal-area and conformal (shape preserving) projections. Again and again the Society has chosen to take a middle route, more or less conformal, more or less equal-area. Perhaps it is no more than a question of institutional *style*.

As we know, Gilbert Grosvenor, president of the Society, thought the Mercator was atrocious. It was his sentiment in 1918 that led the Society to the Van der Grinten in the first place. Grosvenor was never completely satisfied by the Van der Grinten either. "While this is an improvement, it is not satisfactory," he said. The Van der Grinten was nonetheless the projection used by the Society for sixty-six years (from 1922 until 1988).

When the Society switched from the Van der Grinten to the Robinson in 1988, its chief mapmaker said, "The [Robinson] projection does not espouse any special point of view and we believe that its compromises are the most reasonable for a general reference map of the world."

This is nearly a reprise of the song the Society sang about the Van der Grinten.

So similar is the rationale it really does beg the question why the Society switched. Was it just that complaints about the size distortions of Van der Grinten had reached too large a volume? Had there been a shift in the way *National Geographic* readers felt about these distortions? Is this why, though the "better" Robinson projection had been introduced in 1963, it took the Society another quarter of a century to decide to replace the Van der Grinten with it?

Overall, the Robinson represents a compromise. From the standpoint of shapes, no significant area anywhere on the map is completely free of distortion. (This is kept minimal along the equator; it increases toward the poles; similarly, it increases toward the right and left sides, as evidenced by the "shearing" or twisting of North America, for example.) As for size, it lacks equality of area.

What the Robinson does, then, is present a "euphanic" map—that is, one that "looks good." Robinson, some-

61

times described as an artist, *has* achieved an aesthetically pleasing visual image.

Perhaps it needs to be acknowledged that this is no small feat, and that "looking good" is a property of map projections as important for many users as the other properties we have been considering.

The Winkel Tripel

Because of the Society's declared enthusiasm for the Robinson, it came as a shock when in 1998 it suddenly dropped the projection it had launched with such fanfare only ten years earlier. The new one was to be the Winkel Tripel.

The Robinson "is a good projection," the Society would write, "because it minimizes size and shape distortion of areas—except in the polar regions."

Yet what could the Society mean by "minimizes size distortion"? An *equal-area projection* minimizes size distortion. The Gall-Peters projection absolutely minimizes size distortion. Perhaps some of the compromises the Robinson made were politically inexpedient as the Society contemplated the new millennium. For example, although the Robinson projection did reduce the exaggeration of Greenland, it also shrank Africa.

Yet minimizing shape distortion is even more problematic. There is only one conformal projection that is capable of showing the whole world, the Mercator. We know how badly the Mercator distorts areas. We also saw in Chapter One the way the Mercator preserves shapes only in a peculiar and confusing way.

Yet as even the Society admitted, when switching from the Robinson to the Winkel Tripel, projections *did* exist more capable than the Robinson of minimizing

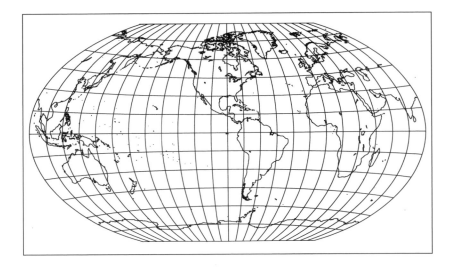

Figure 42. *This is the "new" projection the Society replaced the Robinson with. Oswald Winkel invented it in 1921.*

shape distortions. The Society stressed, in fact, how much the "new" projection—actually invented by Oswald Winkel in 1921 and extensively used in European atlases—improved shapes.

Again one may wonder why the adoption took so long. Seventy-seven years had elapsed since Winkel introduced it. Be that as it may, the Society explained that, "The shapes of countries and islands on the Winkel Tripel look better for three technical reasons": the lines for the poles were shorter, the parallels were equally spaced, and the angles of intersection for parallels and meridians were closer to 90°.

The Society gives an example of this improvement. On the globe, Greenland is about twice as long as it is wide. On the Robinson projection, Greenland is about as long as it is wide, a significant distortion. "On the Winkel Tripel Greenland is one and a half times as long as it is wide—not perfect, but Greenland's shape looks good, and its size distortion is moderate."

The Elusiveness of Shape

Recall our earlier discussion of shape, about how shapes can be true locally, yet not true overall. We used the example of drawing a face on different projections. Now we need to deal with what shape is.

It seems so obvious, but if you try to put it into other words, it turns out to be hard. Our dictionary says shape is "the outline or surface configuration of a thing; a contour, form," and, "the contour of a person's body, figure." This just substitutes "outline" for "shape." The question remains: what is it about one shape or outline that allows us to tell it apart from another?

The problem is not new. What, for instance, is the shape of Italy? The ancient Greek geographer, Strabo, wrote, "it is not easy to describe the whole of Italy under any one geometrical figure. Some say it is a promontory of triangular form . . . but a triangle, properly so-called, is a rectilinear form, whereas in this instance both the base and the sides are curved. It is better to confess that you cannot exactly define ungeometrical figures." Yet we know Italy when we see it.

A modern geographer, William Bunge, says that "Shape has never been measured," and though he said that forty years ago, it remains essentially true today.

This is especially true of things like faces. What is the shape of a face? Somehow faces can change, as between laughing and crying, yet remain the same. The shapes of faces change with the perspective, too. A face seen from below is not the same as when seen from above or head on. That head-on face is not the same as the face seen in profile. Faces are particularly different seen far away or up close. Somehow we can even recognize the shape of a face that has been distorted, as in a caricature. Yet we do not say that the person's face changes.

Mapmaker Borden Dent makes a similar point about the shapes of mapped areas. He calls shape an elusive element:

If we view a continent on a globe so that our eyes are perpendicular to the globe at a point near the center of the continent, we see the shape of that continent. However, the shape of the continent is distorted because the globe's surface is falling away from the center point of our vision. We can view but one point orthogonally [that is, from directly overhead] at a time. If we select another

63

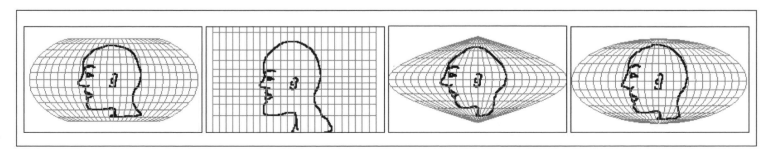

Figure 43.

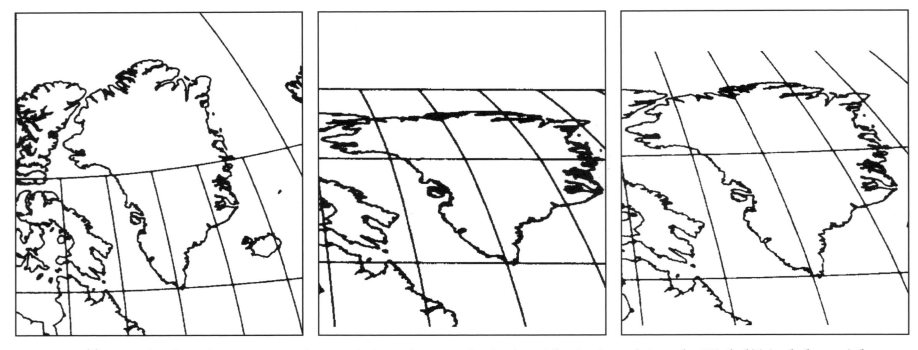

Figure 44 *Greenland is about twice as long as it is wide, says the Society. The Society claims the Winkel Tripel shows it best. What do you think? The Van der Grinten, left; Robinson, center; Winkel Tripel, right.*

point, the view changes, and so does our perception of the continent's shape. The point is that shape depends on our point of view.

Winkel made his projection as though there could only be one view of the globe. Therefore, it had to be as broadly satisfactory as possible. It had to portray no truth to be able to demonstrate some transcendent truth. (Where have we heard that before?)

His projection—the third of three he described in 1921—is literally a middle way. It is an arithmetic mean—an average—between two older projections: the equirectangular and the Aitoff projection.

The equirectangular is also known as the plate carrée or plan chart. It is one of the oldest and simplest projections known. For a long time it was believed to have been invented by Eratosthenes, who is better known for his attempt to measure the circumference of the earth. As it is usually presented, the parallels and meridians of this cylindrical projection make squares, crossing each other evenly at right angles.

To the casual eye this equirectangular projection looks somewhat like the equal-area projections descended from Lambert, except that there is less distortion toward the poles. From this it may be deduced that it is not equal-area, and indeed it is not, though the scale is constant along every meridian.

The Aitoff, introduced in 1889 by David Aitoff, a Russian, is itself a modification of an earlier projection, the azimuthal equidistant projection.

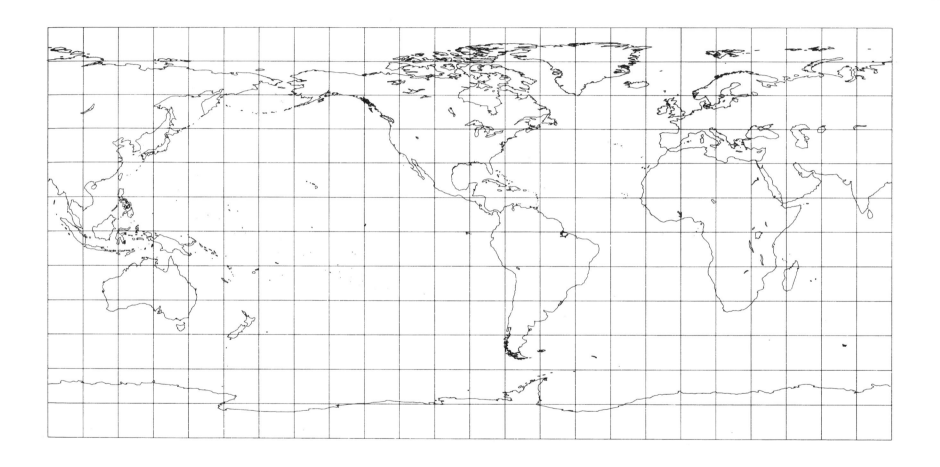

Figure 45. *This is a modern reconstruction of the equirectangular projection. It may be the simplest projection of all. It is also among the oldest. Given the square graticule, you could draw this map on a sheet of store-bought graph paper.*

The azimuthal equidistant projection is said to have been used by ancient Egyptians for making star maps, but its first certain use dates only to the 15th century. An azimuthal equidistant projection, as we know from Guelke's map of the world centered on Toronto (our first example in Chapter Three), displays true scale and direction along any line drawn through the center, but both of these properties are lost in Aitoff's complicated modification.

Winkel took the arithmetic mean of these two earlier projections—the equirectangular and the Aitoff—to derive his Winkel Tripel. The projection is neither equal-area nor conformal. Parallels and meridians are curved. So is the outline of the map, and indeed this is a characteristic of all three of the projections the National Geographic Society has used for its world maps.

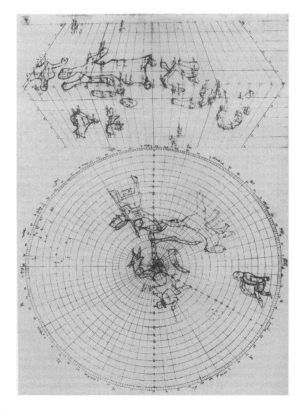

Figure 46. *Conrad of Dyffenbach used this polar azimuthal equidistant projection in 1426 to map the stars instead of the earth. This projection may be as old as the equirectangular projection on the previous page. As different as they appear, they are the basis for the Aitoff projection, to the right .*

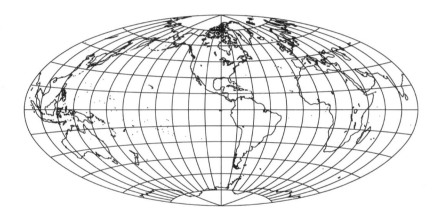

Figure 47. *David Aitoff's modification of the ancient azimuthal equidistant projection.*

The Winkel Tripel is a good example of the way people have again and again tried to achieve the perfect projection.

From our point of view it is like trying to achieve the perfect image of a face. The important thing about a face is its mutability, the way it changes. What is wonderful about faces is the way they can suddenly break

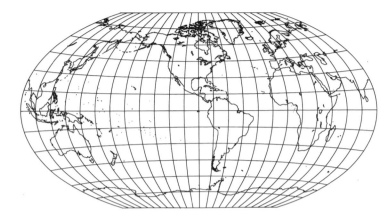

Figure 48. *The Winkel Tripel is an average of the ancient equirectangular and the Aitoff, itself a modification of the ancient azimuthal equidistant projection. The quest for the perfect projection never ends!*

into smiles, or frowns, light up with new thoughts or compose themselves into portraits of sympathy. We enjoy seeing the faces we like in motion, coming toward us, turning, now looking up from a chair, now down from a ladder, profiled against a stormy sky or bathed by the light of the rising sun. There is no "best" view of a face.

As there is no "best" view of a face, there is no "best" view of the earth.

Imagine saying of a portrait that in not attempting to show any special truth it gives perhaps the best over-all picture? What would this mean, the average of a smile and a frown? Frozen between laughter and tears? And one might say yes, if you have to have just one picture, then . . . perhaps . . .

Why Settle for Just One Point Of View?

But we do not have to have just one picture. We can have, we *do* have, many. There is no reason for maps all to be on the same projection. The ceaseless repetition of a single projection tries to convince people that "this" is what the earth looks like. But the earth does not look the way any individual projection makes it look.

Each projection is but a glimpse, a facet of the earth's reality. As with faces, it is the multiplicity of views that nurtures understanding, especially that essential understanding that the big picture is beyond the grasp of any solitary view.

Is this an attack on the Winkel Tripel? Not at all. In fact we are heartened that when the National Geographic Society made the switch to the Winkel Tripel in 1998, it did not raise its usual defense that the best image of the globe was one that took no point of view at all. Instead it merely claimed that the Winkel Tripel was good: "We chose the Winkel Tripel because it is a good representation of the world—not a perfect representation—but a good representation. The only perfect representation of the world is a globe."

This too is an opinion from which one can dissent. A globe *may* be free of distortions of size, shape, distance and direction. But a globe is awkward to handle, very small scale (or where larger scale, *very* awkward to handle), and hard to use.

Have you ever tried to measure something on a globe? Getting a string or tape to lie down is hard enough, without the globe spinning away from you! It is easy to say the globe is perfect until you try to use it:

It is not easy to provide space large enough [on a globe] for all of the details that are to be inscribed thereon; nor can one fix one's eye at the same time on the whole sphere, but one or the other must be moved, that is, the eye or the sphere, if one wishes to see other places.

Ptolemy said that about globes eighteen hundred and fifty years ago.

Imagine what a fighter pilot might think about trying to use a globe in the cockpit of a jet! Don't you think Ptolemy and the pilot would agree about the imperfections of the globe?

The lesson is: *a thing's appropriateness depends on the use to which we want to put it.* As we said before, a shovel is great for digging in the ground; a spoon is just about right for eating soup. The important thing is not to confuse them.

The Winkel Tripel may be a good representation of the earth, but it depends on the purpose. What do people use political maps of the world for? Don't they compare places and, among other attributes, their sizes? We do not know—not really—but if this is among the things people do, then the Winkel Tripel might not be all that appropriate.

On the other hand, the Winkel Tripel will not be terribly misleading either. *It is the quest for perfection that misleads.* The solution is always to have several maps at hand, to understand the ways in which they differ, and to compare and contrast.

Reactions
Learnings
New Insights

Questions

Q: This upside-down stuff hurts my head! Aren't you just playing silly games with this kind of stuff?

A: Silly? No! Rather, we've challenged your assumptions.The more attached you are to YOUR way being right, the harder a time you'll have with new perspectives. Sorry about the headache, but we did warn you— in the introduction—that you might even change your views about things!

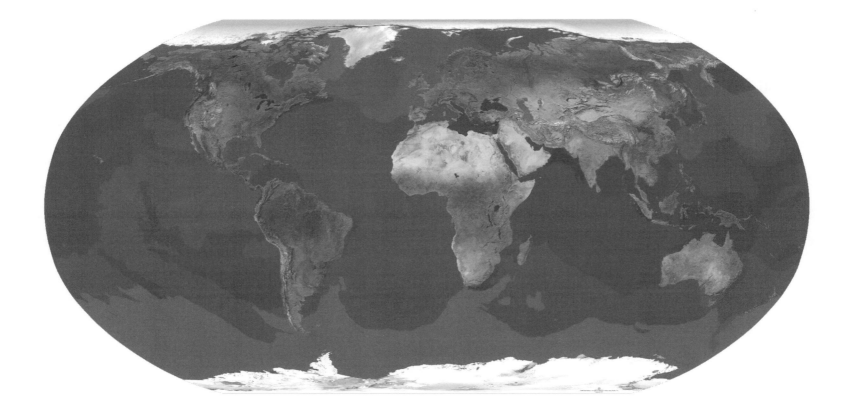

Figure 49. *Like Hockney (See Figure 50), the artist and mapmaker Tom Van Sant collaged this portrait of the earth,*
The Earth From Space. The image contains over 900 million pixels.
Van Sant's method erases the traces of his multiple sources to focus attention on his subject.

Van Sant's GeoSphere Map

Here is a map that really makes clear what a map is. Precisely because it looks like a photograph.

Indeed, this is a map that wants you to accept it as a photograph, to buy it as the real thing. It presents itself as what all the dreamers struggling with the perfect projection have always striven for: the perfect image of the earth.

Something about this image almost succeeds in convincing you that this is the earth. The description is part of the reason for this. Everyone refers to it as a portrait. It carries all the associations we have with the idea of a portrait:

A subject sits for the camera. The shutter snaps. When the film is developed what you have is an image of what was sitting in front of the camera. The connection is that tight. It is the real deal.

In our discussion of the Winkel Tripel projection we talked about this idea of portraiture, questioning the pretense of capturing—in a single image—what in fact is an endlessly shifting reality. Even so, we did not question the chain—light, lens, film—that underwrites photography's claim to capture something *real*.

The map in hand plays with this understanding. It exploits this familiar idea of a portrait to pass off what is in actuality a collage.

This is not immediately obvious. Everything about this image conspires to prevent such a reading. There are no seams. No lines acknowledge the presence of paste, of overlapping paper.

But a moment's reflection convinces us it has to be a collage.

If not, where could the camera have been standing?

Not on the moon, surely! The image of the earth rising over the moon's rim is quite familiar. Only a part of the earth is visible—not even an entire hemisphere—and what is visible is swathed in cloud.

Certainly not on a man-made satellite then? The camera would be too close, and could have caught only a part of the earth.

72

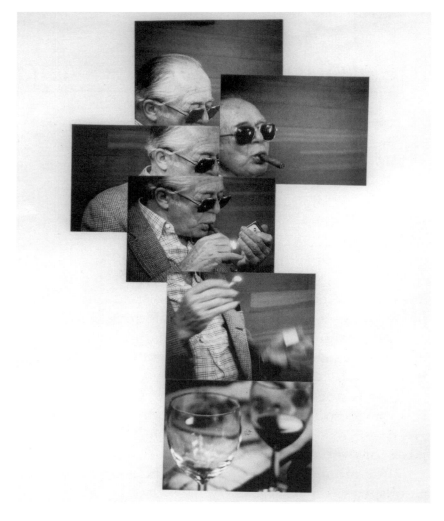

Figure 50. *The photocollage portraits made by the British artist David Hockney not only 'capture' their subjects, they redefine what portraiture might be. This portrait of the Hollywood director, Billy Wilder, captures some of his 'endlessly shifting reality.' Hockney's method draws attention to the multiple photographs from which it was composed. Van Sant's GeoSphere map does the same thing as the Hockney collage, except that hidden from the viewer is the fact that it is an assembled image.*

Which is what it did. Indeed the camera caught no more than a fleck. The camera was on a satellite. The image *has* been collaged.

In any case, how else could it have been made? Is this not precisely the problem we have been looking at in projection after projection? How to give, that is, how to capture, the whole globe in a single view? Wasn't it eighteen hundred and fifty years ago that Ptolemy pointed out that in order to capture the globe either the globe had to move or the eye did. One or the other. There was no way to see it all otherwise.

Except on a map.

So this has to be a map. The photographs—millions of them—were collaged together (it was done by computer which is why there are no seams). They were stretched and squeezed, as invariably the surface of the

Figure 51. *The earth as seen from the moon. Its most prominent feature is the clouds, erased in the Van Sant portrait.*

globe has to be if it is to lie flat on a piece of paper, into the Robinson projection.

Making It Look Right

It could have been any projection. Other projections of this image exist. Indeed, the imagery was gathered for the GeoSphere *globe*, which is the best way to appreciate it. However, the Robinson was very popular when this image first appeared. At that time it was the National Geographic Society's choice for mapping the world.

We didn't look at the history of the Robinson in the last chapter, but its story is instructive. It models the history of projections in general.

In a way the story starts with John Paul Goode, a mapmaker active in the first half of the 20th century. He strongly opposed using the Mercator in schools—as so many have—precisely because its distortions of size can be so misleading. As an alternative, Goode developed a number of interrupted projections. His Goode's homolosine is the most well known. (We have already referred to it in Chapters Two, Three and Four.)

Goode interrupted the sinusoidal projection in 1916. Later that year he also interrupted the Mollweide. Both were equal-area projections. Finally, in 1923, Goode combined these two interrupted projections. The goal was to retain the equal-area properties while

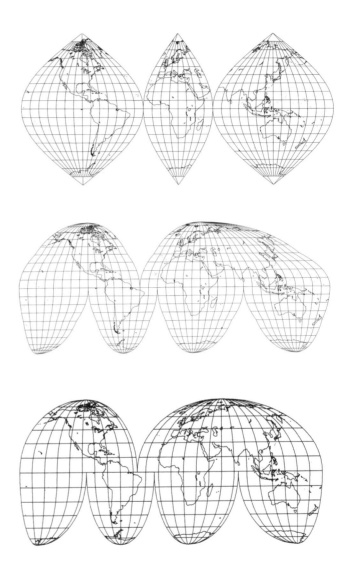

Figure 52 *In an interrupted projection each landmass gets its 'own' best projection, so to speak. The price paid for this is having gaps between the lobes. Top: An interrupted sinusoidal; Middle: Goode's interruption of the Mollweide; and Bottom: his combination of the best of each in his Goode's homolosine projection.*

getting rid of some of the distortions in shape and scale.

These goals should sound pretty familiar by now. Goode's strategy amounts to a way of making a compromise projection by "collaging" together the best bits of other projections.

Interrupting projections allows mapmakers to continually "recenter" the projection around each land mass (or, should oceans be the subject, each ocean). Each of these "recenterings" creates a lobe or, in the case of the Dymaxion, a square or hexagon.

The gains in fidelity of shape and scale are offset by the gaping discontinuities that break up or "interrupt" the projection. Places that are next to each other on the globe can be far apart on an interrupted projection. This is especially true with the Dymaxion.

On projections like Goode's the effect is less disconcerting than it first appears.

And it is hardly unique. As we have pointed out before, *this loss of adjacency occurs at the edges of every map*. After all, the places farthest from each other on a map, at the left and right edges of the sheet, are right next to each other on the globe. In this way *every map* interrupts the globe. Interruption is *what it means* to roll the globe flat.

On the other hand, the Goode's homolosine is interrupted all over the place.

A problem arose when publishers who didn't understand the map filled in the gaps to make it continuous. This made the oceans huge. This was not the first time that a map had been misused—think of the Mercator—but the enormous oceans raised a firestorm of criticism.

Ultimately Rand McNally, the publisher of one of these filled-in maps (you would have thought they should have known better), responded by hiring Arthur Robinson to find a projection with all the strengths of Goode's homolosine but none of its weaknesses.

Do we need to say that no such a projection exists? Of course Robinson could not find one.

That is when Rand McNally hired Robinson to *create* a projection, one that would not be interrupted; that would minimize the shearing that "disfigured" the sinusoidal; that would minimize distortions of area and scale; and that would have a simple graticule (like that of the Mercator or Peters or, for those of you who have really been paying attention, the equirectangular).

Robinson's approach to the problem was unique. Instead of wallowing in the wake of five hundred years of efforts to project the graticule using simple formulae or simple geometrical constructions, Robinson worked by trial and error.

The point was less to do something elegant than to make a map of the world that *looked right*. Robinson strove to reduce the bloated exaggerations of the Mercator and similar projections. At the same time he worked to avoid the shearing seen in projections like the sinusoidal, and the stretched-out look of projections like the Gall-Peters. In the last chapter we discussed the extent to which Robinson achieved these objectives.

The public didn't take to the projection when it was introduced. It was too used to the Mercator, which it continued buying. It wasn't until the National Geographic Society made it their projection of choice

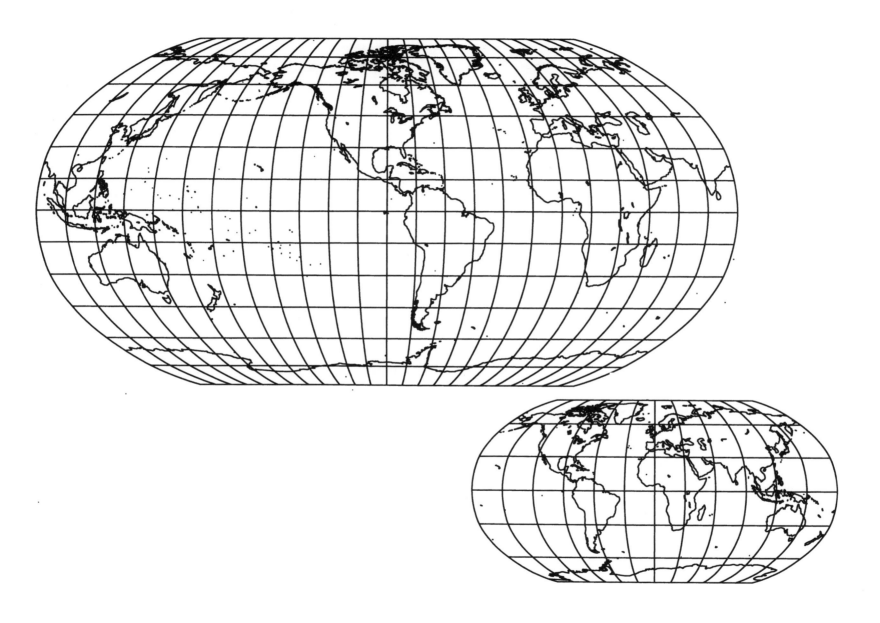

Figure 53. *Arthur Robinson tried to work out a grid that would make the map 'look right'—make it look like the earth is supposed to look. But how is it supposed to look?*

76

for world maps that the Robinson acquired any popularity.

Ironically the same thing had happened to the Mercator when it was introduced: it took decades for sailors to acclimate themselves to the novel projection. Once people get an image of the earth in their heads, it is hard to persuade them of the advantages offered by another point of view.

Another name for this reluctance is prejudice. To work against it, keep as many perspectives in play as possible!

The Portrait Is a Map

So: the Van Sant "portrait of the earth" on page 68 is a map. Its millions of satellite images have been squeezed and stretched into Robinson's projection, which itself squeezes and stretches the globe onto a plane. But the images have not just been squeezed and stretched. First they had to be selected from a vastly larger number of satellite images.

Why was this?

In the first place, because a photograph of the earth would have included the clouds that are so characteristic a feature of the planet. Despite the pretense of this image—*of maps in general*—to show the earth

Figure 54. *Clouds may get in the way of seeing what is important or clouds may be* **what** *is important. Here we see, among other clouds, Hurricane Luis. Luis killed 17 people and caused $2.5 billion worth of damage. In the photo the eye is due north of Puerto Rico.*

the way it is, more often than not maps fail to show the clouds. Clouds "get in the way" of showing ... *what?* What is it that is so important that the clouds must be sacrificed to show it?

The land. The map is about the land. Were this a person, he or she would be naked.

This is neither good nor bad, desirable nor undesirable. The truth is that sometimes people wear clothes and sometimes they do not. Yet there is no sense that you have to get out of your clothes to have your portrait taken. Quite the opposite in fact.

So: less a portrait of the *earth* than a portrait of the *land*. And yet among the cloudless images, only half could be selected. The problem this time?

Night.

Not that there is nothing to see on the unsunny side of the planet. Indeed, the night world is every bit as fascinating as the day world. For humans it may be more so. The satellite view of the earth at night is an image of human activity, of the parts of the world that have been electrified, of the oil fields where "waste"

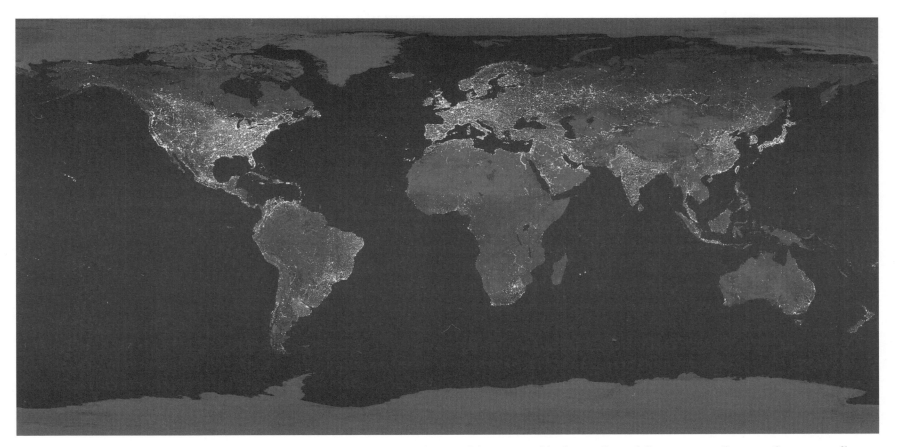

Figure 55. *The day world is one of reflected sunlight. The night world is one of light radiated from street lamps, from gas flares, from field-burning in preparation for next year's planting. It is as interesting as the day world, and more exclusively human.*

gas is flared off, of the smoldering fields of peasant farmers getting ready to sow their crops.

So, the *cloudless daytime* view of the land squeezed and stretched into the Robinson projection. Anything else? Indeed. From the cloudless daytime images only those taken at the height of summer have been selected. Unlike the world, where at any time less than half the world is in summer, here in this "portrait" it is summer all over. In effect, this is a map of maximum vegetation coverage.

Figure 56. *A plant hardiness zone map is actually an image of the seasons sweeping north in the spring, from Gurney's Seed & Nursery Co 2001 Spring Catalog. It is a map of when you can plant and when you can't. Unlike the Van Sant, it is not summer all at once.*

The Map Is a Painting

Finally let us acknowledge that the data streaming from the satellite are not colored. In fact, some of the "information" received was outside the visible light range. Color had to be applied. The mapmaker, Tom Van Sant, "chose colors that would give a realistic view of the physical earth."

Chose colors? What else could this mean than that this map is a *painting* of the earth? The planet sits for its portrait, but not before a camera. Or rather the painter does use a camera but he uses the camera the way a painter uses a brush. The painter sets the pose (without clouds), arranges the lighting (no nighttime shadow), selects the season (summer), and then at the console of his computer, picks realistic colors.

Is there anything wrong with this?

No. It is a perspective, a point of view.

But as *one* point of view it is not necessarily better.

It is not superior, just different and interesting. In its own right, it is both valid and valuable.

The problem with the map—with every map—lies in its connotations. Let's take an illustration. If you looked up the word *mother* in a dictionary, it would say, "female parent." Certainly that would be accurate, but the definition fails utterly to reflect the rich emotions that attach to the word. If the simple "female parent" said it all, what would happen to the greeting card industry? Surely *mother* is one of the most meaning-loaded words in the language!

These distinct levels of meaning are known as *denotation* and *connotation*. To *denote* is to make a precise and objective statement, to define. To *connote* is to recognize the feelings and attitudes that cluster around a word.

To *denote* is to make a precise and objective statement, to define. To *connote* is to recognize the feelings and attitudes that cluster around a word.

Precisely that difference applies to every map. In the case of the Van Sant, what we have is a Robinson projection of a map of cloudless daytime summer land collaged from carefully selected satellite imagery color-coded by hand. That is denotation.

In the realm of connotation, however, it is the world . . . *as it really is!*

In the realm of denotation the Mercator is a conformal projection on which lines of constant compass bearing are straight lines, and therefore of great utility to navigators.

In the realm of connotation it is the world . . . *as it really is.*

In the realm of denotation the Peters is an equal-area projection.

In the realm of connotation it is the world . . . *fair to all peoples.*

Understanding that every map is a projection that gives up some aspect of global reality in order to present what it shows—and that is otherwise endlessly selective—should free you to see *through* the connotations to the denotative maps that support them.

And so in turn to be able to scrutinize the *connotations*.

Understanding that every map has a point of view and serves a purpose should free you to take the point of view that serves *your* interest.

Minard's Map of the Russian Campaign

One reason it is so important to understand how to read maps is that maps can carry so much information. According to Edward Tufte, an expert on visual communication, highly detailed maps like Van Sant's can cram as much as 150,000 bits of information into *a square inch*!

An average US Geological Survey topographic quadrangle carries over 100 million bits of information. *That is in excess of 250,000 bits per square inch!*

Maps can do more than show where places are too. Take a look at this map of Napoleon's invasion of Russia on the next page. Compared to the maps we have been looking at, what strikes you?

This map was developed by an engineer who refused to be boxed in by the cartographic conventions of his day.

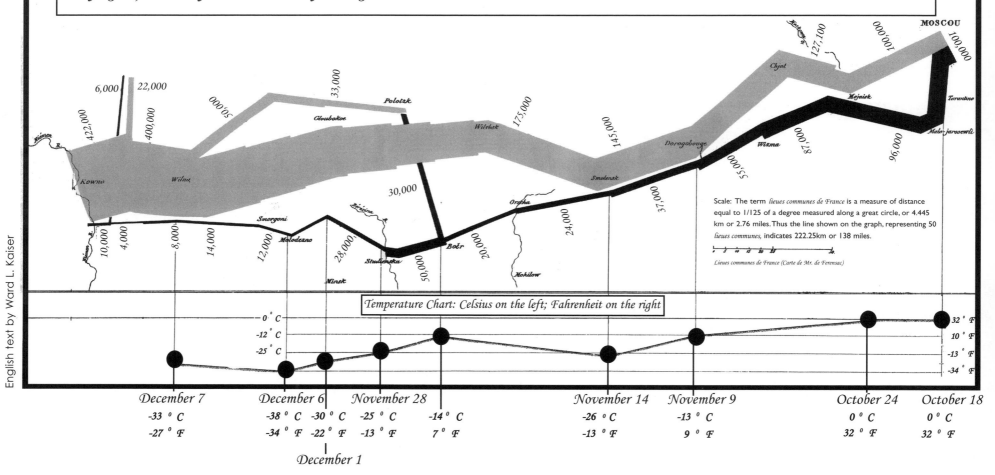

Figure 58. *Minard's map of Napoleon's Russian campaign.*
This graphic has been translated from French to English and modified to most effectively display the temperature data.

Of course, for starters it is not a map of the world. But then—although maps of the world are what we have been concentrating on—*most* maps are not of the world. They are of a part of it, like this one.

This is a map of a part of the Russian Empire early in the 19th century. The river at the left is the Niemen, then part of the border between Russia and Poland. Moscow lies at the map's right. The ever dwindling bands between them represent the size of Napoleon's army, the lighter part at the top shows the march *to* Moscow, the darker part beneath it, the infamous *retreat*.

The numbers along the band spell out precisely what the map so powerfully suggests, that in invading Russia, Napoleon lost an army. To contemplate the possible richness of map data, consider the variety of questions this simple one enables you to answer:

- How many soldiers did Napoleon lead east from Poland?
- How many died en route to Moscow?
- Where did they die?
- How many soldiers died during the retreat from Moscow?
- Where did they die?
- When did they die? (The dates appear along the bottom of the chart.)
- What was the effect of the weather on the retreat? (The temperatures during the retreat are indicated along with the dates.)
- How many soldiers did Napoleon lead back west across the Niemen?

So rich is the graphic you can almost hear the soldiers of the Grande Armée with their despairing cries at the disastrous crossing of the Berezina River in retreat. (Observe how markedly the band thins where it crosses the Berezina.)

Given the temporal dimension, as you follow the invasion from left to right and the retreat from right to left, are you moving through space (over miles or kilometers)? Or through time (over months)? Or are you doing both? How does this differ from the way you usually read a map, or does it?

The map was designed in 1861 by Charles Joseph Minard, an engineer working for the French government. Minard had developed a technique for mapping statistical data such as canal traffic (with which he was professionally concerned) and the volume of wine exports.

Here Minard wanted to apply his technique to Napoleon's Russian campaign of 1812. The band begins broadly, representing the army's full strength of 422,000 men. The band narrows as it moves to the right, both from the Niemen to Moscow and from June to September.

Napoleon did take Moscow, only to learn the meaning of "hollow victory" since the city was a lifeless shell. Minard's keying of the retreat to temperature makes it clear why so many soldiers froze to death. It is a subtle way of informing the reader that besides the Russians the French faced a second enemy: the weather at its rawest.

Minard also showed the movement of the troops deployed to protect Napoleon's flank and rear.

This map actually does *not* possess the data *density* of a US Geological Survey topographic quadrangle. It is not nearly as rich as Van Sant's map. It is, none-the-less, a powerful graphic. Edward Tufte says the Minard map is perhaps "the best statistical graphic ever

82

drawn." In part this is attributable to its simultaneous plotting of six variables: the army's size, its location in the two dimensions of space, the direction of its movement, and the temperature and dates during the retreat.

But it is also attributable to the importance of the rich, coherent story Minard tells. On one level his map is no more than a flow chart in space. But on another level Minard may have been making an argument, graphically driving home a point. Perhaps his point was political, or social or humanitarian or anti-war, but it is hard to escape being moved by the magnitude of the French losses.

Not all maps display movement like this, or are as moving, but most maps *do* display an abundance of complex data in forms that are comparatively straightforward. Like Minard's, maps *do* tend to be about significant, useful things.

The Black Diaspora

It is important to acknowledge how much information maps can carry, but it is no less important to acknowledge how maps *shape* that information.

Lewis Carroll, who wrote *Alice in Wonderland* and *Alice Through the Looking Glass*, wrote another book called *Sylvie and Bruno*. In this work Carroll imagines people who are uneasy about the way maps function. They hold that maps leave out some things that just might be important. Logically, then, a good map must continue to add information until it shows *everything*. The map these people end up creating is—you guessed it—as large as the area itself. If it were unrolled, it would *literally* cover the area.

Absurd? Of course! But the silliness makes a serious point. A map is not the world. (We already have the world.) Nor is a map a virtual world. Rather, as we said early on, to create a map is to abstract from the world those factors deemed important, and display them in a form that allows them to be useful.

To create a map is to abstract from the world those factors deemed important, and display them in a form that allows them to be useful.

We hope you have kept this sentence with you. It comes as close as we can manage to defining a map.

Take a look at the map on page 83. It is a black and white reproduction of a map in color. How accurate does it seem to you? How reliable? How well does it show shapes, comparative sizes, distance, directions? Could you navigate by it? On a scale of 1-10, how would you rate it?

Catherine Petit made this map to show major routes followed by slave traders in the 17th and 18th centuries. If you were given that same assignment, what information would you consider it important to include? What would you choose to leave off as irrelevant or distracting? In what ways do you suppose your effort would look like Petit's? How might it look different?

Think about this, for instance. You may know that Atlantic slavers often sailed along a triangular route. They would carry manufactured goods from Britain to West Africa. Once their holds were emptied, they would fill them with human captives. In what came to be known as the Middle Passage (the second side of the triangle), they carried the slaves—those who survived—to places like Brazil and the southeast coast of North America. Here they would pick up sugar, cotton and other raw materials to carry back to England's factories.

Would you have shown this larger triangular trade route? Or followed Petit's lead by simplifying the map to show the slave routes alone?

Had you shown the rest of the triangular trade, would you have felt compelled to also show other important contemporary trade routes? From an economic perspective, it is hard to make sense of the triangular trade without them.

Where do you stop?

Perhaps you also know about the significant routes Arabs operated during these centuries, routes

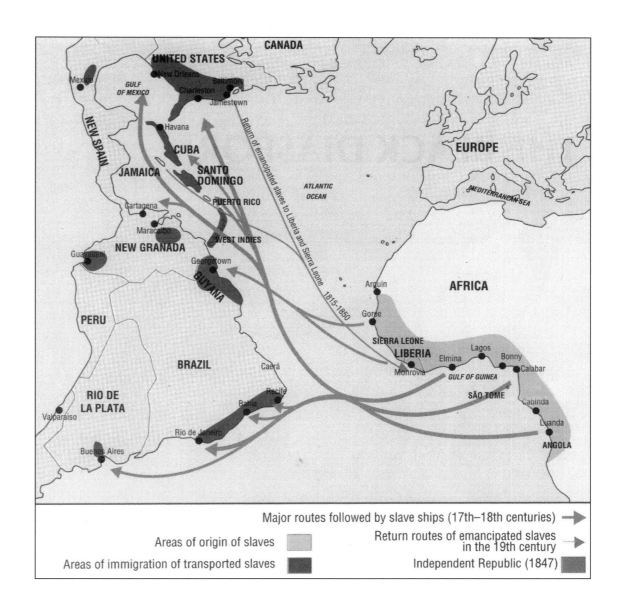

Figure 58. *Catherine Petit's map of the major routes of ships involved in the Atlantic slave trade during the 17th and 18th centuries.*

84

that ran West African slaves north across the Sahara. Perhaps you feel these too should figure in a map of major slave routes of the 17th and 18th centuries.

It depends on your purpose, doesn't it?

Think again about what we said above about maps being abstractions from the world of those things deemed important. How does one decide what is important? How does one decide what is useful and relevant, and what should be omitted?

In this case Petit made the map for the *Penguin Atlas of Diasporas*. Its editors make the case that diaspora peoples are those who as a minority manage in one way or another to perpetuate their identities as a people. The editors feel that those Africans carried to the Americas have done this. They feel that those transported north across the Sahara have not.

The map illustrates the section in the atlas on the black diaspora to the Americas. The map is not trying to cover the world, nor 17th and 18th century trade, nor even all 17th and 18th century slavery.

The London Underground

What strikes you about the map on page 85? Granted that London's Underground is a marvel of engineering, do you really imagine the tracks are as neatly laid out as they are shown on this map? Do they really take careful aim at the compass points? Are there in fact no detours around obstructions, no swings away from a straight line to make an important stop? What about distances? Do you think the map is drawn to scale? How could you tell?

If you were using the Underground for the first time, what other information would you find useful?

How about which stop to get off at for Westminster Abbey or Buckingham Palace? Or which stations provide wheelchair ramps and accessible restrooms?

Henry Beck, an engineer for the London Underground, made the first version of this map in 1931. His initial draft elicited sharp criticism. In his words:

The design was duly submitted, but, to my surprise and disappointment the very idea of a 45- and 90-degree schematic treatment was thought to be too "revolutionary": my Underground map was handed back to me and that, it seemed, was to be the end of it.

From a mapmaker's perspective Beck's drawing could be understood as no more than standard practice. As we pointed out in Chapter One when mapmakers just hit the main points, ignoring, say, all the tiny twists and turns of a coastline, they call it generalization. Beck's map is a supreme example of *generalization*.

For some, however, Beck's simplification of the network to horizontals, verticals and diagonals was the least of the problem. In order to display the dense inner core of the system with the same clarity as the sparser outlying portions, Beck had to distort the map's scale.

This too is something that from a mapmaker's perspective is not inherently alarming. Yet there were those in the beginning who called Beck's map inaccurate, misleading, distorted, even part of a propaganda plot. (Has any new view of reality escaped this accusation? We are thinking of the Mercator, the Robinson and especially the Peters.)

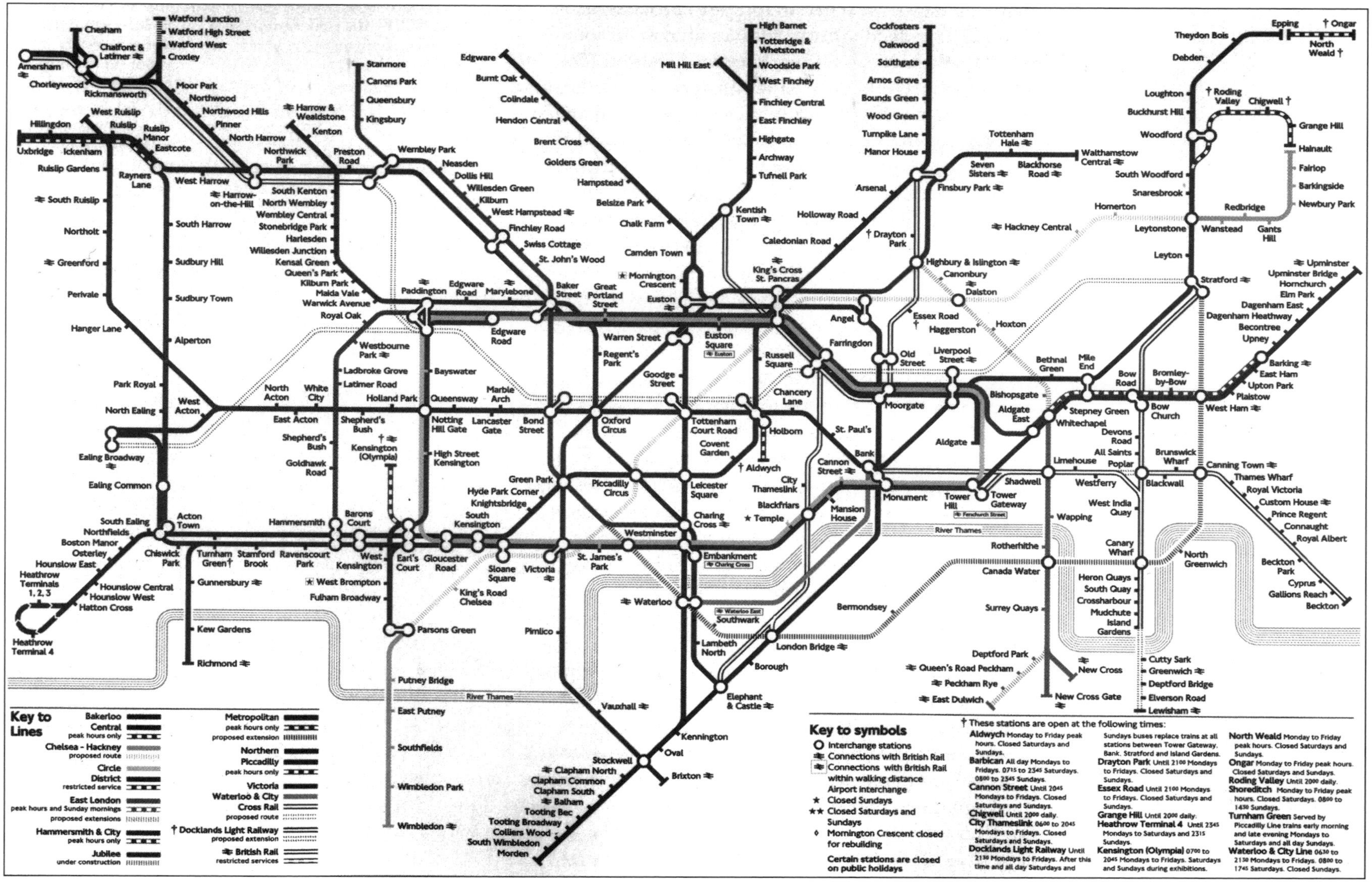

Figure 59. *Henry Beck created the original version of this map of the London Underground in 1931. It has helped millions of Underground users ever since.*

Beck's map was easy to understand. It was clear and comprehensive. It told users what they needed to know without overloading their circuits with confusing detail. It was a highly suitable replacement for the chaotic, "more accurate" maps previously available.

It was soon embraced by ordinary people who needed to know how to travel from one part of the system to another. The map has served uncounted millions of Underground users in varying forms from 1933 to the present. At the same time it has become an icon: an outstanding example of saying more with less.

Cartograms: Weird or Creative?

Take a look at *this* map on page 87. Once again it is a map of the world, but . . . *which world?*

What has happened to the Pacific Ocean? And the Americas? It is as if they had drained the bottle Alice drinks from in *Alice in Wonderland* that makes her shrink. India, China and Indonesia, on the other hand, look as if they had eaten the cake Alice nibbles that makes her grow.

And *what* has happened to the familiar shapes of the continents and countries? There are no curves. Canada has been squashed flat as a pancake!

Can this map possibly be accurate?

When we asked this question before, we had in mind the sizes and shapes of the *land masses* occupied by countries on the globe. But a country is more than territory. It is also people.

We have said that every map gives up some aspect of reality to present another. This map gives up territory to present people.

On this map the size of each country is proportional *to the size of its population.*

You may not be able to make out the little squares in our reproduction, but they are easy enough to see on the original poster. Each square represents a million people.

Looking at the world this way is a revelation. From the perspective of population, China is the biggest country in the world! India is not far behind. For a real shock, compare Indonesia with the United States. Compare Mexico with Canada.

Africa is not as big as the news sometimes makes it. *Asia* has half the people in the world!

Which map would you say is fair to all peoples now, the Peters or this one? Or are they both fair, in different ways?

It depends, doesn't it, on our point of view?

A map like this is called a *cartogram*. An ordinary dictionary says a cartogram is a way of presenting statistical data geographically. Minard's "Map of the Russian Campaign" presents statistical information geographically, and so does Petit's map of "The Slave Trade." In the most general sense, both are cartograms.

More often, though, the term denotes a map, like ours here of "The World's Most Populous Countries," in which the statistical data is presented *by a distortion of the familiar geographic base.* Instead of making countries proportional to the size of their territory, they are made proportional to some other characteristic: here to their population, in our next example on page 89, to the amount of carbon dioxide they contribute to the atmosphere.

Cartograms can be made by distorting the size of any areal unit: states, provinces, watersheds, counties,

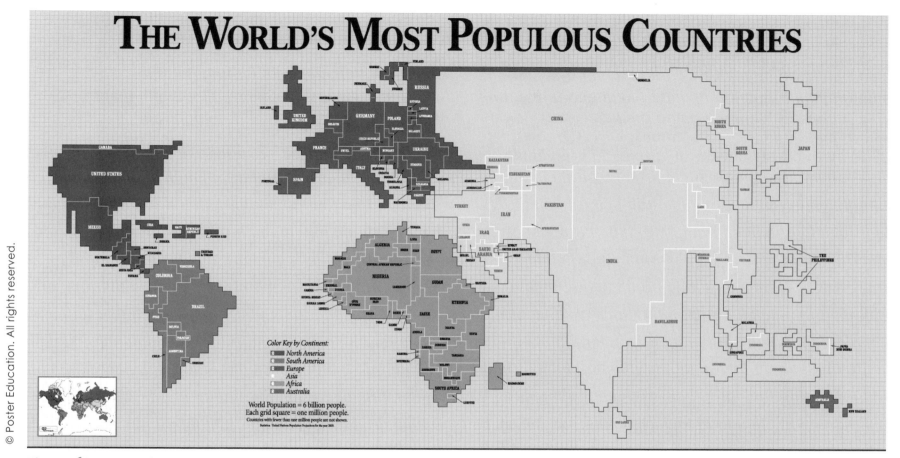

Figure 60. *A population cartogram showing size of country in proportion to population size.*

cities, precincts, wards, you name it. They can be made proportional to the population, to the numbers of members of political parties, to the numbers of birds of a given species, to the percentage of people buying airline tickets to specified destinations, to any statistic.

When the size of a country or other area shifts, the relationship of its parts also changes. For example, in Figure 60, Canada shrinks, so the distance between its northern extremities and its southern border shrinks

even more. Therefore cartograms may also play with shape and scale. In this way cartograms combine features of Minard's and Petit's maps—their display of statistical data—with the distortion of shape and scale on Beck's "Underground" map.

Making sense of cartograms depends on the reader's familiarity with the geographic base. In this way cartograms resemble caricatures. You cannot "get" a

88

caricature unless you are familiar with the figure it refers to.

On the next page is another cartogram. It is a figure from Dan Smith's *The State of the World Atlas* (1999, Penguin Paperback, $11.99). This map makes the size of each country proportional *to the percentage of carbon dioxide* it emits to the atmosphere. Carbon dioxide is the most significant of the world's "greenhouse gases," those responsible for global warming.

If each person on earth contributed equal amounts of carbon dioxide to the atmosphere, this map would be indistinguishable from the "The World's Most Populous Countries." We can see that it is anything but.

On this map it is Germany, Japan and the United States which seem to have snacked on Alice's growing cake, and Africa which has sipped from her "Shrink Me" bottle. Middle America (Guatemala south through Panama) has disappeared altogether, along with the Caribbean (except for Cuba) and much of Africa.

Some of these vanished countries simply have *very* small populations; but other countries with small populations nonetheless loom relatively large on this map (like the Arab Emirates), and others are quite disproportionately large. These countries have populations with *high individual emission rates*, and on the original map these rates are shown in color.

The color variations, more difficult to discern in our black and white reproduction, display four classes of individual carbon dioxide emission. Now we can understand why the United States seems so bloated: *each* of its inhabitants contributes more than 20 tons of carbon dioxide to the atmosphere each year. In China, each person contributes less than five tons a year.

Since most carbon dioxide is emitted by power plants and internal combustion engines, this is effectively a map of the disproportionate use of electricity and cars by some of the world's peoples.

Maps such as these, which illuminate sharp disparities in resource availability and use, raise profound questions of social equity.

Such complicated relations are often hard to put into words, but on maps like these they can be seen—and grasped—with comparative ease.

Like Beck's Underground map, a cartogram is another way of saying more with less. From these cartograms, everything has been eliminated but the distinction between land and water, and crude caricatures of the world's countries. What the maps blazon forth are statistics that catch important features of our lives.

This really *is* the world. It is the world seen, not through eyes in space, but through those of a policy analyst. It is a different world, but it too is ours.

Other intriguing images in cartogram form can be found in *The New State of the World Atlas* by Michael Kidron and Ronald Segal (1991). Many statistics that would appear as dull and boring in a table or list are brought to life when illustrated on a cartogram. When you see the representations of spending on arms versus health care, you have a richer perspective on how we treat global priorities. For example, there were more than 46 million people under arms worldwide, . . . over five times the number of doctors.

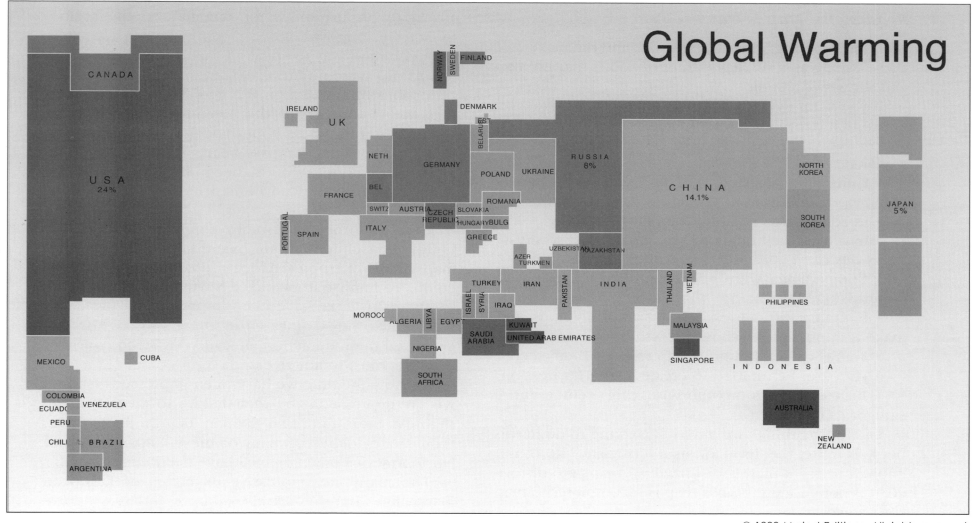

Global Warming

Figure 61. *Another cartogram. This one shows each country's emissions of greenhouse gases. It is basically an indicator of energy consumption.*

Reading the Map is Our Problem

What Van Sant, Minard, Petit, Beck and the makers of these cartograms so clearly understood is that no map can show everything.

If you want to put a complicated subway system on a card that people can fold up and put in their pocket, almost everything has to go. But things can go for many reasons:

• Limitations of space, as in Beck's case, affect many mapmaking decisions.

• In some cases reliable data may be lacking.

• In others the budget may be inadequate to satisfy every desire.

• Some things were not asked for by those who commissioned the map.

• Technical difficulties, as in world projections, may make it impossible to show everything the way it is.

• Things can be left off a map to keep them secret.

• They can be omitted to create a false impression.

• Bias, conscious or otherwise, can exclude entire categories of existence.

One of the things we have been trying to do in this book is raise the level of map criticism. It is not enough to say a map is distorted; all maps are distorted. It is not enough to say a map is incomplete; no map shows everything.

What is essential is to use your knowledge of the omissions and distortions to understand the map's purpose.

Case in point: during the commercial rivalry between the young Australian cities of Melbourne and Geelong in the mid-19th century, a map was produced by a firm in Melbourne. It made Melbourne out to be the closest major city to the gold fields and other attractive opportunities for migrants to the region. In fact, Geelong was closer.

A common way to speak of this is to say this map's distortions were intentional. They were, but so are the distortions of a Mercator or a Peters. The difference is that the distortions of the Mercator and Peters are intended not to mislead but to achieve the higher purposes of constant compass bearing and equivalence. There is, by contrast, no higher purpose to justify the distortions of the Australian map. Its only purpose is to mislead.

Here's another case, more ambiguous but clearly highly consequential. In examining selected early maps, maps of tropical Africa prepared by Portuguese colonial administrators and of North America prepared by the British, we have been impressed by the detail with which they delineate the topography, by the precision of their depiction of every twist and turn of even the most minor rivers.

At the same time we have been impressed—should we say depressed?—by their failure to give even the slightest indication that human beings lived there. From the evidence of many of these maps, Africa and North America might as well have been uninhabited.

The maps are impressive examples of European mapmaking. But they are also—importantly—windows into European minds (and their inherent biases).

Those who commissioned and those who drew those maps are no longer here to speak for themselves. Were they, they might well defend their work. They might claim some sort of technical objectivity or retreat behind the barricade of "disinterested science." They might claim to be mapping only the permanent features, not the ephemera of humankind.

Such "explanations" side-step the question of why they considered streams more important than settlements, hills more vital than people.

It leaves open the possibility that by depicting these territories as people-free, the mapmakers made it easier for colonial administrators to treat native peoples as nonentities. So they could occupy or usurp or give away or sell or plunder the land on which the people lived, as though it *belonged* to the Europeans. Why bother to consult people who literally—according to the maps—weren't there?

It would be in keeping with the ancient and human tradition of overlooking the more troublesome aspects of events like genocide, enslavement, exploitation, and forced resettlement of indigenous peoples.

Was the only purpose of the colonial maps to mislead? Who is to say? One thing is clear: they did not go out of their way to correct any misimpressions they created.

This confronts us with the issue of complexity. The problem is that most maps are made with many, often competing, purposes in mind. Few are as simple as Henry Beck's map of the London Underground. More often maps are as complicated and multidimensional as Tom Van Sant's desire to show the earth as it really is.

In the end, the problem of seeing through the map is not the mapmaker's, it is yours and ours.

What do *you* think?

Now that we have reached this stage in our book, we hope you are more willing to take responsibility for critiquing a map image you are presented with. Our goal throughout this book is to stimulate your critical thinking, to have you uncover the hidden bias found in every map, and to understand how maps influence and shape your view of the world.

Reactions
Learnings
New Insights

Questions

Q: Seems like part of your motivation for writing this book was to challenge my prejudices. Is that true?

A: Bingo! The more readily you can accommodate many maps' points of view, the more you will expand your consciousness to be able to see things from other peoples' perspectives. Here's where training in map skills has a direct consequence for your flexibility and open-mindedness in lots of other human endeavors.

Throughout these pages we've illustrated and reiterated one principle: that the images on our walls and TV screens, in our atlases and in our minds, powerfully shape our beliefs, attitudes and daily actions. How we view our world and how we map it make a difference. Far from being just an academic exercise, we're talking about how conventions and habits affect our perceptions every day of our lives.

Let's consider a few examples.

Why Do Clocks Run Clockwise?

Ever hit a home run? Then you certainly know enough to run the bases counterclockwise. Horses run the track counterclockwise; so do Olympic runners. Skaters skate counterclockwise.

Clocks, on the other hand, run clockwise. What lies behind that simple fact? Mere coincidence?

A moment's reflection convinces us that we *could* read a clock face the other way around—with the "1" where the "11" is, and so on. So it is not a case of

Figure 62. *Ever wonder why clocks move clockwise?*

mechanical or logical necessity that clocks look the way they do.

94

Henry Fried, a prominent horologist (meaning not a clock-watcher but a student of time measurement) provides a simple explanation.

Fried says that in the days before people had clocks, they relied on sundials. In the northern hemisphere the shadow cast by the pointer rotated in the direction we now call clockwise. So it seemed perfectly natural or "right" for European designers of early clocks to copy that motion.

But only in the northern hemisphere does the shadow move that way; south of the equator it moves in the opposite direction. If clocks had been invented "down under," (recall what we said about the "What's Up? South!" map of the world) clockwise would probably mean *the exact opposite* of what it now means. So it is the geographical location of the clockmaker—not an innate law of time or even of psychology—that determines the meaning of a common idea we use every day of our lives.

Our Maps and Our Self-Centeredness

Think again about the map called "It's Your World, Toronto." It literally sets the people of that city at the center of everything.

In a way we may find that amusing. Everybody *knows* that Toronto is not the center of the world! How could it be? A globe has no center on its surface. Yet in some signifi-

Figure 63. *Toronto-centered equidistant map by Guelke.*

cant way Toronto *is* the center—for the people who live there.

Indeed, *we all* put ourselves at the center. No matter where a person stands on the face of the earth, she or he effectively occupies the very center of the world. It would be physically impossible to look out at the world from any pair of eyes except one's own, from any position other than the actual one where the observer is standing. An appropriate map of that person's world would not be a Mercator or a Peters or a Winkel Tripel, but an azimuthal projection centered on that individual's position.

This fact of life shows itself throughout history. Let's consider examples from a variety of times and places.

Belly Buttons and Worldviews

Twenty-five hundred years ago, on a small clay tablet the size of a hand, the Babylonians inscribed the earth as a flat disc. Babylon stood at the center.

The early Greeks were similarly convinced that they lived at the center—they called it the navel—of the world. According to one of their myths, the god Zeus released two eagles at opposite ends of the earth; they met at Delphi. So Delphi came to be, for them, the place of supreme or central importance—that place where, for example, there could be communication between humans and the gods, through an intermediary known as the oracle. Today a decorated stone known as *omphalos* (the navel) is on exhibit in Delphi's museum. It was discovered in the temple ruins in that city. There it had served for centuries as

Figure 64. *Some scholars consider this the oldest map of the world we have. It shows the homeland of its creators, the Babylonians, as the center of the world.*

a visual reminder to people that their city occupied the central position in the world.

Far from Greece, in what is now Peru, the Incas called Cuzco, their capital, the navel of the earth. How their maps showed this we cannot be sure; Cuzco

was almost totally destroyed by fire in 1536, in the Incas' struggle against the Spanish conquistadors. But those writings that have been preserved into modern times clearly tell of a city of impressive design and complexity, which both emotionally and in name carried the designation, Navel of the Earth.

About four thousand miles north from Peru, we find Atitlan, Guatemala. Here, the Tzutujil people (indigenous Mayans) called their lakeside village Rumuxux Richiliu, the Belly Button of the Earth. So many places, so many navels!

Over centuries the Chinese have thought of themselves as living in "the central kingdom." Their maps of course reflected that. In map after map the Chinese capital sits at the very center. The rest of China surrounds the city, then a sea encircles China . . . the remainder of the world is relegated to an outer ring of land. Thus two very human principles get clear expression through the mapmaker's art: the centrality of one's own people and the marginalizing of all other people.

A Spanish Christian bishop named Isidore read in his Bible, "This is Jerusalem; I have set her in the midst of the nations," (Ezek. 5:5) and so concluded that the city of Jerusalem stood at the geographic center of the world. That was in the seventh century; since Western Europe's history intertwines with Christian history, European maps tended to follow this "Jerusalem is the belly button" model for centuries.

But wait—does this not contradict our thesis: that people place *themselves* at the center of their world? Europeans did not, after all, live in Jerusalem!

At a more profound level, however, it supports the theory: so strong was the people's identification with

Jerusalem that they could fairly be said to "live" there—emotionally if not physically. They looked out on their world *as if* they were citizens of Jerusalem.

Muslims similarly saw the world through their own eyes. A twelfth-century mapmaker, Al Idrisi, placed Mecca rather than Jerusalem at the center. Africa, Al Idrisi's home continent, with its significant Muslim population, was enlarged until it occupied more space than all other continents combined.

One further example out of many possibilities: a map of the world recently published in Japan sets Tokyo close to the center. The map is not Euro-centered; for people living in Japan it's *here*-centered.

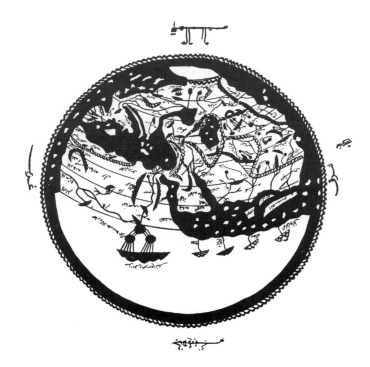

Figure 65. *Islamic cartographer, Al Idrisi, created this map in 1154. He placed Mecca at the center.*

The vantage point of the viewer has once again become the central point of the map. And why shouldn't the Japanese see themselves at the center of the world? The rest of the world has been doing it all through history!

What else do you notice about this map?

We've hidden some hints—if you need them—elsewhere on the next page!

In our time Arno Peters, among others, has called attention to what he calls "the Europe-centered character of our view of the world." He points out that many maps using Mercator's projection have located Western Europe close to the visual center. This reflects *our* cultural history: Western European mapmakers have strongly influenced our understanding of the world. This is evident not only on maps created in Europe and North America but throughout the world.

Did you notice the Japanese map is on the Mercator projection?

In addition, those many maps Peters calls "Pseudo Mercators"—maps using the Van der Grinten are prime examples—reduce some of Mercator's distortions without correcting its Eurocentricity or nothern-hemisphere bias. Of all of these Peters says, " . . . they no longer fit into our post colonial world, in an epoch of international understanding, universal equality of rights and worldwide communication."

But there is more, much more. What does this say to you about the influence of Western ideas and European-sourced images? From the physical to the metaphysical, from the geographical reality to the mental or perceptual reality is but a small step. Ask, for example, how a section of the Asian continent came to be known by us as "the Far East." Certainly the people

Hint #2: what projection has been used?

Hint #1: where is north?

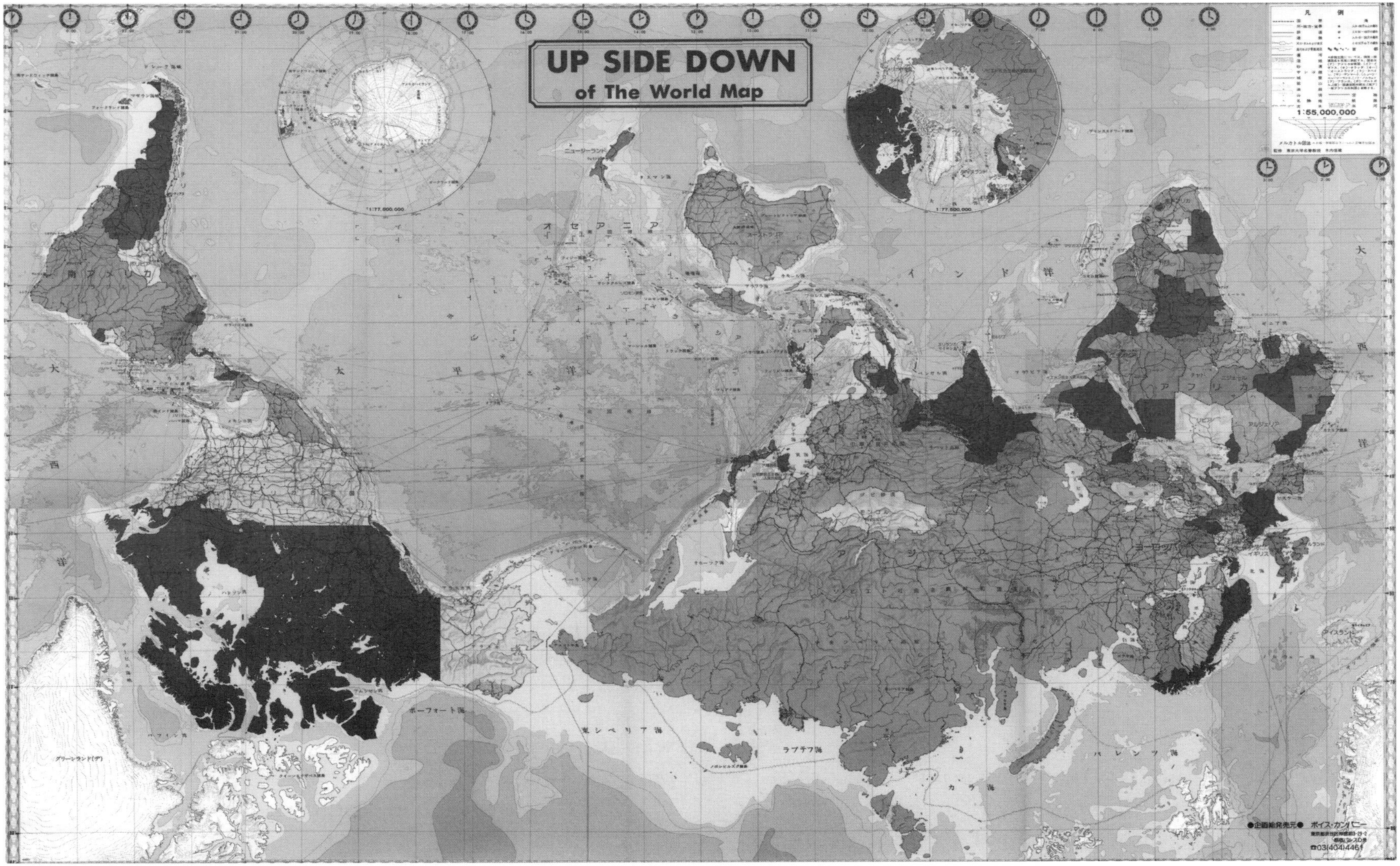

Figure 66. ***Tokyo is near the center of this map.***

living there didn't call it that; for them, it wasn't "far" at all—it was simply "here," as is well demonstrated in the Tokyo-centered map of the world. But to the people of northern Europe, including adventurers, colonial administrators and mapmakers, it was both far-off and to the east, so what was more natural than to call it the Far East? Similarly, the British Foreign Office developed the term "the Near East" for the region around the eastern end of the Mediterranean, generally the same part of the world that Americans knew as "the Middle East." The point is: the name revealed the observer's vantage point. If you had drawn an equidistant world map centered on, say, London, "Near East" and "Far East" would seem pretty logical. But the terms do slide from being descriptive of geography to being symptomatic of a particular (and often insular) mindset.

This slippage is not restricted to diplomats and military planners or Europeans; it appears to be universal. In individual terms, it becomes self-centeredness. Applied to one's nation it becomes chauvinism—one's own country, whatever it does, is right. Applied to "our kind of people" we call it ethnocentrism. In other contexts it can transform into racism, cultural myopia, parochialism and xenophobia. What all these have in common is that we view the world from one perspective only: that place on earth where we happen to stand.

Arno Peters, among others, has pointed to the connection between traditional maps (including, but not limited to, the Mercator) and our European or "northern hemisphere" sense of superiority. These feed off each other: when people stand at the center of their world, they understandably create maps that reflect

that fundamental fact of life. On maps, when they see "their place" at the center of things rather than off at the margins, their feelings of superiority are enhanced.

Psychologists call this egocentricity. Social scientists call it perceptual bias. Theologians call it the sin at the heart of things. The human tendency to think of one's country or culture as superior is pervasive. It prevents us from cultivating compassion and empathy for those "other"/"different" people we share our planet with. When we see things only from one cultural perspective it becomes all too easy to see others as inferior, or even to make those people we don't understand into our "enemies."

But naming the problem is not the same as dealing with it. In producing his map, Arno Peters reduced the dominance of the northern hemisphere and scaled its bloated size down to realistic proportions. To large numbers of people, accustomed to seeing "their" part of the world front and center and very prominent, this was uncomfortable in the extreme. After all, who enjoys being downgraded?

Maybe these people felt—and still feel—like Louis XIV of France did when presented with a new and more accurate map of his country. An earlier map of France (drawn in 1679) was set down, and a new map (based on astronomical tables and published in 1693) was superimposed upon it. The "new" country was 20 percent smaller. What a shock! This prompted Louis to complain that he had lost more territory to his mapmakers than he ever had to his enemies.

"Orient" and "Occident"

Everybody knows the terms "the Orient" and "the Occident"—right? They are, after all, in pretty common use. Our dictionary mentions such meanings for Orient as: *the east (a direction), the East (as in Asia)*, and *in the direction of the rising sun*. For Occident, not surprisingly, it gives *west (the direction), the Western Hemisphere, the direction of the setting sun*. Obvious, perhaps.

Now suppose we are on the rim of Asia—let's say we're standing on the eastern shore of Japan. Where, in this case, does the sun "rise"? Is it not across the Pacific, in that part of the world we call the West, the Occident? And where, in that context, does it "set"? Would you not agree that it goes down over Asia—the area of the globe that Europeans traditionally refer to as "the East" or "the Orient"? Sometimes east and west refer to directions, sometimes to places. And the places never stay put. Can you see how it begins to get confusing, even contradictory?

What, then, do these terms really stand for? Do they refer to precise, definable locations? Or are they just convenient expressions that serve as long as we don't examine them too closely? Our underlying purpose in helping you to "see through maps" is to encourage your critical thinking. When you hear a term like "Orient" or see an image (on any projection), we hope you will now begin to ask: "What assumptions are built into the concept or image I'm presented with?"; "What other points of view might provide an entirely different 'take' on things?"; "How might this appear to someone raised in an entirely different culture or country?"

99

east and west. . .
directions?
or
locations?

An Image So Powerful It Changed the World

You've heard of the princes of Serendip, perhaps. They were constantly finding something valuable while they were looking for something else. From their fanciful story comes our word *serendipity*.

Christopher Columbus could have been one of them. He was looking for a certain place—Asia—and stumbled on another—the Americas.

But *why*? What led him to suppose he would find "the Indies" out there, anyway? The story combines fact and legend, honest error and deliberate deceit, high purpose and sordid behavior, mapping mistakes, high skill, and a good measure of pure, dumb luck.

Maps and Globes That Got It Wrong

Believe it or not, Figure 67 is a serious map of the world. It wasn't tossed off from memory by a flunking grade-school student, but by a renowned mapmaker, Martin Behaim. Look first at Europe ("Europa"). Would you agree that it's recognizable? Certainly compared to other areas on the map, it approaches broad-stroke accuracy. By contrast, how accurate is his Africa? What hypothesis would you set forth to explain this drop-off in accuracy? Where you might expect to see the Americas on a "normal" map, what stands out? "India" is of course quite prominent; "Cathaya" was his term for China, and "Seylan" for Ceylon, now Sri Lanka.

Scholars generally give Columbus high marks as a navigator. Although he was familiar with celestial navigation (reckoning by the stars), he preferred to rely on his compass and mathematical calculations. On his first voyage he left Palos, Spain, then headed southwest to the Canary Islands ("Canaros" on this map). After some needed repairs to two of his ships, he sailed pretty much due west, holding to his compass bearings even when his readings off the North Star didn't agree. He simply decided the North Star must have shifted, so disregarded it.

Just as he chose one navigational method over another when they conflicted, so—if we are to believe some of the stories that have grown up around the man—he kept two sets of distance calculations. The real one was for himself; the false one, for the crew's information—or disinformation. He deliberately underestimated how far they traveled each day, afraid his men would lose heart if they knew how far they had sailed without sighting land. Indeed, about thirty days out, according to legend, he did face a reluctant crew.

When he rejected steering by the stars, Columbus also set aside other aids commonly used by navigators: the quadrant and the astrolabe. Tossed by the waves, his little (by today's standards) ship was too unstable to permit reliable readings from these instruments. Columbus even relates in his log how he fell overboard once trying to use his quadrant, and shelved it for the rest of the trip.

But luck and navigational skill were with him: he had hoped for a voyage as short as twenty-one days, but even thirty-six to India did not seem unreasonable. "Figures don't lie," we might imagine him saying, secure and smug in his accomplishment. "I figured on thirty-something days to get to India. It's now thirty-six days, so this has got to be India."

And the prevailing world-image of the day offered further support. Look at it: where else would Columbus suppose he had landed? So the term

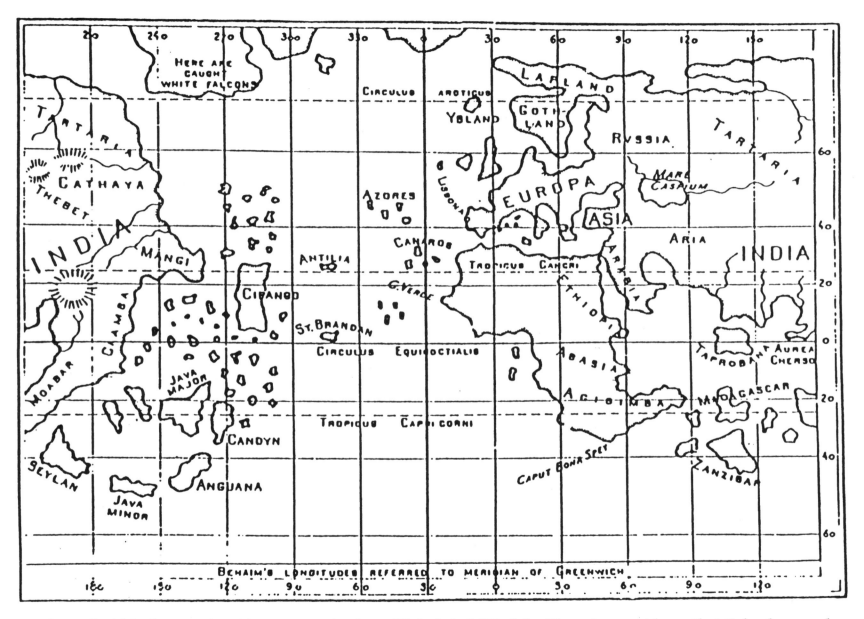

Figure 67. *This flat map is a Mercator projection of Behaim's 1492 globe. There is no evidence that Columbus used this globe—and he certainly never saw this map—but it graphically portrays how some Europeans in 1492 perceived their world. It was that perception, that image, which may have convinced Columbus he could reach the Asian continent in a reasonable period of time by heading west across the Atlantic.*

"Indian," which he mistakenly applied to the people he met, has lingered with them ever since.

But if Columbus was mistaken, the originating error surely belonged to the makers of maps. Take Behaim as an example: he underestimated the circumference of the earth by about 25 percent. The Greek philosopher-scientist Eratosthenes had calculated a circumference of the earth as early as 228 BC, but mapmakers like Behaim and adventurers like Columbus either didn't know about it, or could not make any more sense of it than we can today.

Suppose Columbus had known the truth: how *very far* it is from Spain to India. Would he have ventured to cross "the Ocean Sea" (the Atlantic) and the vast Pacific anyway? More pointedly, would he have found a crew willing to risk their lives on such a foolhardy venture? That, of course, is a matter of speculation. One thing is sure: for a voyage of that duration, he and his crew would have needed a lot more food and water than they actually had on board, or they would have died of hunger and thirst before they came to land. That's where Columbus and crew were just plain lucky: they *happened* on land—land they did not know existed. Finding that land both boosted their morale and provided the food and drink that saved their lives. And of course finding a "new" land changed both their maps of the world and the world's future.

Once again, how people viewed the world made a difference. It always does.

In Conclusion

Maps are powerful images. They affect us consciously and unconsciously. They tap into our sense of adventure. When we pick up a map we become explorers investigating lands that represent new horizons to us. Many of us have reverence and awe for maps, or are at least attracted to them. Our job in this book has been to integrate a healthy respect for the power of maps with a critical perspective on how they can mislead and misinform us. The effective map user will look at the map knowing that both points of view are true.

Reactions
Learnings
New Insights

Alternative Views of Columbus

Most North Americans look up to Christopher Columbus as a national icon. All around us are reminders of his status: a dozen cities and towns proudly named Columbus spread across the country; to these add institutions such as Columbia University, areas as big as British Columbia and as small as Columbus Circle in New York City. Let's not forget the annual celebration of Columbus Day in most states. In the U.S.A., Columbus is one of only three persons to have a national holiday all to himself, the others being Martin Luther King Jr. and Jesus of Nazareth.

Not everyone, however, holds Columbus in such high regard. For an alternate point of view, here are three very different perspectives:

James W. Loewen's award-winning book, *Lies My Teacher Told Me*. New York: Simon and Schuster, 1995, p. 70. On the web at: **http://www.uvm.edu/~jloewen/index.html**

The National Council of the Churches of Christ in the U.S.A says " . . . What represented newness of freedom, hope and opportunity for some was the occasion of oppression, degradation and genocide for others."
More info on the web at: **http://www.indians.org/welker/faithful.htm**.

See Ronald Wright's provocative *Stolen Continents: The "New World" through Indian Eyes*. Toronto: Penguin Books, 1992.
More info on the web at: **http://www.kckcc.cc.ks.us/ss/stolen.htm**

Before he set sail, Columbus had an image of the world in his head. It may have been wrong, but he acted on it. From his action came results both good and bad. The exact mix of good and bad varies widely among sincere people.

You, like all the rest of us, carry with you an image of Columbus. It may be right or wrong; it may well be incomplete or fanciful, critical or laudatory. In what ways does the popular image shape our sense of who we are as a people? Write your answer below.

Questions

Q: Are you suggesting that it is wrong to put your own country at the center of a map?

A: No, we're not saying it is wrong. In fact, it is very human and natural. We just want to make you aware that when you create a map, or use a map, with your country in the center, you reinforce a worldview that can limit your understanding of the rest of the peoples of our planet. What we want to do is "jostle" your thinking, so that you can begin to imagine how things look from other perspectives.

How Many Purposes?

Throughout we have referred to the purposes of maps. Every map, we said, is a purposeful selection from everything that is known, shaped to the mapmaker's end. Often, we cautioned, what is missing from the map is a clue to the purpose the map is serving. You should use the map that serves your purpose. Only given the purpose can a map's rightness—its *truth*—be assessed, we insisted.

We illustrated our point with maps whose purposes included:

• Helping us get around town (the Duke security guard's map of Durham);

• Helping sailors get where they wanted to go (Mercator-based maps and charts);

• Helping sailors figure out their shortest routes (maps based on the gnomonic projection);

• Showing areas in their true proportions (maps based on the sinusoidal, Lambert cylindrical equal-area, Mollweide, Gall, Hammer, Eckert II, Eckert IV, and Peters projections);

• Sharing the mapmaker's knowledge (maps by Mark Fisher, Andrew Kent and Jessica Kim and the Medieval T&O map in Figure 36 on page 50);

• Showing areas in their true proportions but with more accurate shapes (maps made with interrupted projections including Goode's homolosine and Boggs eumorphic);

• Showing distances from a chosen point (Guelke's centered on Toronto);

• Showing the world as "spaceship Earth" (Fuller's Dymaxion map);

• Showing the world so that it *looks* right (maps based on the Van der Grinten, Robinson, and Winkel Tripel projections);

• Shaking up our point of view (the "upside-down" maps, the nighttime view);

• Showing the world "as it really is" (Van Sant's map);

• Preparing people to deal with disaster (the map of Hurricane Luis);

106

• Helping people know when to plant (the map of hardiness zones);

• Explaining things, raising consciousness (Minard's map of Napoleon's Russian campaign, Petit's map of Atlantic slave trading routes)

• Helping people navigate a complex subway system (Beck's map of the London Underground).

Helping, sharing, showing, explaining, shaking up . . .

You can probably add scores, maybe hundreds of purposes to this list. Some that come to mind, even at this level of generalization, include *possessing, claiming, legitimizing, naming, managing, directing, telling, forbidding, controlling* and *taxing*.

How about: *building identity?*

Institutions everywhere use maps to build identity. The millions of highway maps the states and provinces give away each year are not just to help people get around. They are also so many million assertions of state sovereignty, so many million invitations to see—or imagine—oneself an Alaskan, an Albertan, a New Yorker.

Images of states abstracted from these maps are emblazoned on coffee cups and uniforms, flags and badges, tokens and emblems. The map becomes a potent way of saying who we are.

Except for the flag and eagle, what is more emblematic of the US than its instantly recognized shape? A similar point might be made about Canada; lots of Canadians who can't remember the words to their national anthem gaze with pride at the outline of their nation.

Now think of the UN. Perhaps you have an image of the UN headquarters building. But more likely the image that comes to mind is a world map within an olive wreath . . . the UN flag . . . an image of the world united in peace.

Yet identity building is not a purpose for maps that immediately leaps to mind.

So often maps are identified with finding one's way, with showing someone how to get around. The first map we illustrated was the one the Duke security guard sketched to show us the way to Angier Avenue.

Maps *are* important for wayfinding. In the parts of the world where cars are abundant, road maps are especially common. Millions of maps have been published to help people navigate the world's subways and bus systems. Maps are found in every ship's pilothouse and every airplane's cockpit.

But as we have suggested, most maps serve other purposes. Few of the maps that appear on television, in daily newspapers and weekly news magazines are about wayfinding. Neither are most of those in atlases and textbooks. They are about building up in our minds an image of the world we live in. The maps in books of fantasy serve the same purpose. They are to help us construct pictures of R.L. Stevenson's *Treasure Island*, of the woods that Winnie the Pooh and Eeyore live in, of the Hobbit adventures in Tolkien's Middle Earth.

Tax maps, political riding or precinct maps, maps of school attendance zones, zoning maps, flood insurance maps are not about wayfinding either. They are about ownership and political control.

Inventorying the world is the agenda of the maps made by geologists, soil scientists, biologists and others.

What a range of purposes! How do maps manage to fulfill them all?

Maps Make Descriptions

What does it take to satisfy these diverse purposes? What, if anything, do they all have in common?

Isn't it that each requires—*demands*—a description of the world that sees the world as a place in which the purpose can be fulfilled? Or if not the world, then a part of the world, your region or county, your city or neighborhood, the block you live on or your lot or apartment.

Sees the world as a place in which the purpose can be fulfilled . . . What can this mean?

Consider a piece of land. It is hard to describe a piece of land without invoking purposes or potential purposes. For instance, we might want to say of this piece of land that it is free of significant human structures. The shorthand way these days would be to say that the land is undeveloped (or underdeveloped or underutilized). But this is precisely to describe—to *see*—the land in development terms. Even if the whole thing were covered in climax forest (which in biological terms is to say *fully developed*) we would still say the land is undeveloped.

Anyway, consider this piece of land. Some of us look out over it and see a patchwork of forest and meadow. There are streams and beaver dams and in the evenings deer along the edges of the trees. Even foxes have been seen.

Others of us look out and see a golf course, a hotel and convention center, speculative office spaces and a housing subdivision. They can see a carrier delivering the morning paper and barbecues on weekend afternoons.

To support the first vision one might map the range of tree and other vegetative species; fox, deer, beaver and other mammal populations; unique ecological features; terrific views and magical spaces.

To support the second vision one might map the density of the nearby population, access to airports and major highways, distances to competing functions, the tax valuation of the surrounding land, and the site's topography and soils from an engineering point of view.

The first map would speak of the uniqueness and value of the land as it is. It would speak of rest and solace.

The second would speak to the need for housing and the increased tax base. It would speak of commerce and cash.

Both maps would be descriptions that turn the land into places where the purposes behind the maps could be fulfilled. The maps would *envision*, they would see the land in the terms of these purposes.

It is exactly what roadmaps do, which see the world only in terms of getting around by car. Roadmaps see the land in terms of this purpose.

We have said much of this before. We said, "Maps are descriptions of the way things are, made to support the human purposes that bring the maps into being."

Maps are a part of the process—part of the *action*—set in motion by that purpose.

They are not independent, standing aside, neutral adjudicators of competing purposes. They are caught up in, are part of the purposefulness itself. A map is a purpose-satisfying device. It is a device for construing

108

Figure 68. *Comparison of land from two perspectives.*
The image on the top is a picture of the Mount Holyoke Range in Hadley, Massachusetts.
The image on the bottom is the development proposed by Bercume Builders, Inc.
A community response to this vision of land use can be found at **www.SaveMtHolyokeRange.com** *or* **http://fomhr.com.**

the world in such a way that the purposed action seems reasonable.

A map is a kind of lens that lets us see what we want to see and put it in a form we can share with others.

Isn't this what the competing views of the world—Robinson's and Peters's and Fuller's—all show? That by using simple mathematical formulas—in effect, a lens—without any kind of lying or cheating or bending the truth, we can pretty much show the world the way we think it needs to be seen?

So that it looks *right!*

Fair to all peoples!

Spaceship Earth!

Each is true. All are different.

The Map Is an Eye

What may be less obvious is how much maps are like eyes. Eyes are standard issue, each pair doubtless unique, but each pair enough like all the others to be effectively interchangeable. People insist, in fact, that the evidence of our eyes is the best evidence there is.

Yet eyes too are subjugated to the human purposes they serve.

Looking out on a common scene, one sees a nature preserve, another a development site. One sees forest and meadows, another the best locations for roads. One sees Nature, the other Culture.

Viewing a common subject, one sees the beauty of the human form, another a naked body. One sees art, another pornography. One sees beauty, the other temptation.

What these examples point out is the responsibility we share as perceivers of the world for bringing the world into being. There are many who have trouble with this idea. They want to believe that the world they know is independent of the way they see it.

It is not!

The world we know—the *only* world we know—*is* in the final analysis dependent on how we see it.

And we are to an amazing degree in control of how we do that.

One way we exercise this control is by closing our eyes to avoid seeing things we do not want to believe. An alternative is to open them up to discover things we do not know. We can keep our eyes where they have always been. Or we can take them to places they have never been before.

If we make an effort to look at everything, and try to take our eyes to new places, the world we experience will be much richer, more interesting, more useful, more complete, more generous, more *real*.

But before we believe this is important to do, we must accept the principle that "seeing" is how most of us bring the world into being. We use our eyes to create the world we see. Maps are an "eye" to the world. The more perspectives we have, the more accurate our vision. "Seeing" is meant literally here, but it can also be interpreted as a metaphor. Even visually impaired people "see" the world, although they rely on their other senses to "shape" or create reality around them. And all of us (some more than others) use our imaginations to call forth visions of the future—the world we want.

110

The Eye Is a Map

One way to begin to accept this is to rethink what we just said, replacing "eyes" and "see" with "maps" and "map."

For instance we said, "The world we know—the only world we know—is dependent on how we see it."

The objection many have to arguments like this is that our eyes seem to give us the world . . . *as it is*, unmediated, fully, with nothing left out. The world seems to be so real we can't imagine what could be missing. We may know that dogs can smell things we cannot, and bees see things we cannot, and bats hear things we cannot, but really, what does it all come to? Even if we accept that it comes to a lot, it still requires a powerful imagination to summon up the wholly different world of these animals.

But now, armed with everything we know about maps, try this: "The world we know—which is the only world we know—is dependent on how we map it."

We know this is true!

Is it ovular or rectangular? Centered on Toronto or the Atlantic Ocean? Is north up or is Australia on top? Does Greenland look bigger than Africa or Africa bigger than North America? Is Alaska long and thin or squat and compact?

Each is different, yet the visions maps present us with are every bit as convincing as those given by our eyes. Like our eyes, maps seem to give us the world as it is, unmediated, fully, with nothing left out. "This is the world," they say.

We know better. We know that every map leaves out almost everything. Even one as detailed as Van Sant's forgoes the night, clouds, seasonality, political boundaries. It fails to show the slave trading routes of the 17th and 18th centuries. It would be useless on the London Underground.

Pushed this far, our complaint is ludicrous, but the point is essential. It is easy to construe as a failure the *seeing* completeness of the world that is given by maps and eyes. Kids fantasize about X-ray vision, but imagine what the world would look like if you could see through everything. How would you keep the layers separate? Things would be so jumbled! How could you pay attention to *any*thing? A map that showed *everything* would be exactly as jumbled, precisely as

Figure 69. *Of course, our hero would actually see right through the robber and his victim, right through the back wall, right through . . . most everything.*

dense, as the world would seem with X-ray vision. It would be useless, and impossible to read.

Eyes and maps present selective visions, tailored to our needs. The needs—the purposes—act as editors or filters or lenses to let us hone in on what is important at the moment. Something in our peripheral vision will cause us to turn our head. We will zoom in, focus. Everything else is, for the moment, *out of the picture.*

Now think about how the Duke security guard focused in on just the streets we needed to get to Angier Avenue. He left everything else out. The Mercator forsakes sizes to give us true compass bearings. The Peters pays little attention to shape to give us correct sizes.

Maps often mislead when we attempt to apply one purpose-tailored vision to another purpose. When we are focused on something off to our side we cannot pay attention to what is going on in front of us. It is how distraction works. Sleight-of-hand employs distraction; it is the stock-in-trade of every magician. Manipulative politicans employ distraction when they declare war abroad to avoid a political scandal at home.

Peters would say the Mercator *distracts* us from seeing, from *realizing*, the importance of the tropics. Certainly it is hard to pay attention to—to think about—size-based relationships unless the map we are looking at is based on an equal-area projection.

Maps make it possible for us to deal with issues like this. They enable us to "see" a world in a way that mere words can never do. The obvious question to ask is, "How would this look on a different projection?"

It is a concrete version of, "How would this look from a different point of view?"

Do you see what we mean?
What do you make of it?

Reactions
Learnings
New Insights

112

Mobile Eyes, Many Maps

In the world of maps we compensate for the selective vision of a given map by looking at others. We have said this repeatedly too: "The best understanding comes from as many views as possible." We said, "The best way to understand our world is to view it through as many lenses as possible, to see it from as many vantage points as we can."

This is another point that may be easier to make in the world of maps, but the eye too compensates for its selectivity.

By being wildly mobile.

This is not a picture one often gets. So often people illustrate how the eye works with a cross-section: an object in front of it is inverted as it is projected onto the retina.

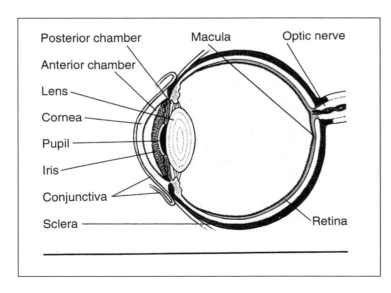

Posterior chamber   Macula   Optic nerve

Anterior chamber

Lens

Cornea

Pupil

Iris

Conjunctiva

Sclera   Retina

Figure 70. *The eye.*

The eye does work this way, and undoubtedly this is interesting. But from the perspective of seeing it is among the least relevant things about the eye: *the most important part of the eye is the feet.*

The most important part of the eye is the feet.

The eye is not a window on the world; not unless the window is in a moving vehicle. That is, things rarely pass before the stationary eye. *The eye moves to get in front of things.* Each eye can be moved left-right, up-down and obliquely by muscles that rotate it in its socket. This socket is mounted on a mobile head. The head is mounted on a mobile trunk. (We don't need eyes in the back of our heads because we can turn around.) The trunk is mounted on a pair of legs, and those on feet. They can carry the eye about anywhere it needs to go.

Needs to go ...

And where *do* eyes need to go? The answer from the world of maps is that eyes need to go all over the place. Isn't this what we have learned? Because the vision of a given map is selective, we have to look at many different maps? That *only* by looking at many different maps can we build up an understanding of the world that in any way approximates reality?

Recall the Van Sant once again. If we could have only a single map, the Van Sant would be a serious contender. It may be as detailed, as informative a map of the world as has ever been made. Because of this, its selectivity does not immediately leap from the surface, though as we know . . .

It is not enough by itself.

We need *weather* maps. We need *daily* weather maps, and maps that show us the long term patterns we call *climates*, and maps to help us understand the even longer term patterns we know as *climate change*.

We need maps of land use too, maps of land use today and maps of land use over time, to track changes, to visualize them against the changing climate.

We need maps of human population, of its distribution now, but also how its distribution has changed, to help interpret the maps of land use and climate change.

We need—

We need many maps. We even need a map to give us a sense of the whole, and certainly here the Van Sant has a crucial role to play. Even this book—which at the outset we called a road map to the world of maps—has its contribution to make.

But no single map cuts it.

And this is what a real awareness of maps teaches. It should teach us not merely which maps to use for what purpose—as valuable and important as that is—but that for the multitude of human purposes we need a wide variety of maps.

Precisely as we need a diversity of maps, we need also to haul our eyeballs everywhere, to take as many points of view as possible, to see things from above and below, up-close and far away, by day and by night.

We need to look with one eye closed and both eyes wide open. We need to set what we see alongside what others see. Having a conversation with those others

about the differences in our world views is the subject of a whole other book.

We Never Said It Was Easy!

All this is easier said than done. The world of maps makes this clear too.

Think about the Mercator for a minute. What *does* its widespread use as a world map really represent? Especially given its inappropriateness and its rejection by so many experts.

Our explanation of its continued popularity acknowledged the attractiveness of its rectangular form and right-angled grid, but stressed the projection's historic popularity among the educated beneficiaries of far-ranging colonial trade and European military power.

It was these, after all, who hung Mercators on the walls of their parlors and had the clout to get them into their children's classrooms. There the projection not only reflected the supposed superiority of the culture which brought it into being, but also offered a view of the world in which the homeland of that culture was substantially exaggerated in size. It was a self-congratulatory view of the world.

As we have said, for the better part of the 18th century, all of the 19th and much of the 20th, the Mercator was accepted as *the* map of the world. The prestige the map had among Europeans gave it an even greater prestige among colonial peoples.

What kind of a world view was this?

It was a class view, one that advantaged the interests of the mercantile class over those of others. Since this class was for much of this time the slave-trading and slave-owning class, it unavoidably supported a racist view as well. Some would claim it still does.

As we further pointed out, once people get an image of the earth into their heads, it is hard to persuade them of the advantages offered by other points of view.

Another name for this reluctance is prejudice. In the case at hand, this is a class and race prejudice.

What can be done about it?

We should not attack the Mercator. We have discussed how the projection is supremely useful for many purposes. Don't blame the projection (or its creator, Gerardus Mercator) for the fact that it has been misused by those who wanted to make it the basis of a world map for purely symbolic reasons.

It was its importance to the sailor, slaver, explorer, whaler, and naval navigator *in regional chart form* that earned the map its fame. Its use as a world map twisted its merits to the goals of class propaganda.

No, do not attack the Mercator, but instead *supplement it*. To work against the undue influence of any one view of the world, keep as many maps in play as possible!

Our point is that this is not always straightforward.

Where interests have intersected to promote one view at the expense of others, where it is the only view one can see, it can be hard indeed to imagine an alternative. If you cannot imagine an alternative there is no reason at all to go looking for one.

Sometimes it is just a matter of moving the eyes, though many social forces work to keep our eyes where they are. Protectors of the status quo have little investment in moving eyes. Who knows what novelties the eyes might see? Who knows what changes might be unleashed?

In the end, though, they are our eyes, and if we actively make the effort to look at everything, and try to take our eyes everywhere, the world we experience will be richer, more interesting, more useful, more complete, more generous, more *real*.

We mean: it doesn't matter how many ways there are to map the world unless you make the effort to turn the next page in the atlas or try a new and different atlas.

Turn the Page

Turning the page, looking at new maps, *moving your eyes to different places*, is the best way to deal with the situation—which is the nature of being human—that we described at the beginning of this book.

There we wrote about eating lunch together but experiencing it differently because we were sitting in different chairs, angled toward each other at the table, so that the background behind each of us was different, so that each of us took in a different view.

None of us will ever be able to sit in more than one chair at a time, or to see the world from more than one point of view at a time. But we *can* switch chairs every now and then. We can *move* the table. Now and then we can even . . . eat dinner at a neighbor's house or eat out at a restaurant!

Once we acknowledge that each chair offers a view which, while partial, is just as true as that from any other, we may find ourselves prepared to acknowledge that the truth exceeds *every* view, that the only way to approach it is from as many views as we can manage.

Having seen through maps we know that each takes a point of view. Sort of like sitting at lunch in *this* chair, or *that*. Knowing this, we then know that the only way to approach *any* truth about the world is to see it through as many perspectives as we can.

Seeing through maps, acknowledging another point of view: these are to admit that truth is found in many places and seen from many angles.

The truth is not something *he* can have, or *she* can have, or *they* can have. It's not something that *you* have a monopoly on either. It's something we can only discover together: by sharing our world view with others and, in turn, taking the time to listen to how others see theirs.

Reactions
Learnings
New Insights

Questions

Q: What is the truth?

A: The truth is found in many places, and seen from many angles!

Maps can be used in ways mapmakers never dreamed of. Here at ODT—the publishers of *Seeing Through Maps*—we've been doing it for years.

ODT is a management consulting and publishing company that focuses on resources related to employee empowerment. Because looking at different map projections causes people to question deeply held perceptions and rethink them, we've used map projections extensively in leadership training, corporate culture change programs, supervisory development classes and cultural diversity awareness programs. The Peters projection, in particular, has proven highly effective in acheiving this goal.

We're not alone in using the Peters and other projections in these ways. Since 1985 the Peters has been used by many international corporations and by some of the largest management training companies serving private and public sector organizations.

The Peters especially has gained widespread popularity as an educational tool in the fields of adult education and human resource development. Adult educators and corporate trainers have recognized the power of the Peters image to dramatically impact their students and enhance their learner's receptivity to new information in a variety of fields.

Adult Education

Theories and models for adult education differ from those for school-age children.

Years of research make clear that adults learn differently. Ken Finn, an organizational development consultant, observes, for example, that school-age children are quite receptive to learning. With effective teaching and the right learning environment, children can be likened to sponges. They soak up knowledge and are eager to acquire new information.

Finn points out how different it is to teach adults, especially when the learners have preconceptions about the subject matter that may be different from what the instructor wants to teach.

While children's minds are like "blank slates"—you can fill in the empty space with things they find useful or interesting—adults's minds are like "full slates."

118

Adults are already sure about how the world works. They have a rich repertoire of life experiences. They have numerous preconceptions about how things are. Because of this it is different (and it may be harder) to teach adults than children.

Before learning something new and different, adults have to let go of their old view. They have "to make room" for the new. This "giving up" is akin to grieving after loss. Finn argues that adult learning is often accompanied by pain, especially when adults are asked to change their world view. It is this feature that drew Finn to Dr. Elizabeth Kübler-Ross's well-known work on coping with death and dying.

Kübler-Ross identified a four-stage process that people go through in dealing with death. Finn discovered that these four stages were identical to the process adults went through when they had to let go of old ideas to make room for new ones. Correspondingly, the four stages of adult learning elaborated by Finn are Denial, Blame, Self-Blame, and Problem-Solving (called DBSP for short).

Denial

At first an adult hearing something that contradicts his or her prior beliefs rejects or denies it: "No! That collaborative performance appraisal model Human Resources just introduced can't possibly work here because _____ [fill in the blank]."

In corporate seminars employing the Peters projection map we have seen mid- and high-level executives, often with advanced degrees in the hard sciences, become agitated and upset upon seeing the Peters image. They'd just shifted into Denial.

Unless a teacher employs strategies specifically designed to deal with the dynamics of denial, learners can resist new information for a very long time.

Leon Festinger's equally well-known theory of *cognitive dissonance* is also relevant here. When humans experience something that disconfirms their view of the world, it sets off an awkward, clammy feeling in the pit of the stomach. This is the feeling of cognitive dissonance. In high states of dissonance, people can deny reality, literally not seeing what is before their eyes. They can dismiss reality, rejecting it as a bizarre fluke unlikely to reoccur.

With the appropriate emotional facilitation and support, on the other hand, learners can shift their old views, let them go, and integrate the new world view into their mental models.

Blame

Among other things, this shifting involves a progression through the further stages of Finn's DBSP model. An adult learner supported through Denial will typically go on to experience Blame. In the case of the Peters this often appears as anger towards schools and the establishment media.

People say things like: "I can't believe the teachers/schools I've had could be so misleading," while others implicate the Mercator projection in a vast European white male conspiracy designed to obliterate the cultural contributions of people of color.

Bob Fleming, Director of Diversity at Harvard Pilgrim Health Care in Boston, uses the maps in workshops for hundreds of employees, and says that parents "get angry that [the Peters] isn't being used in the school system." They become upset that their children are still being exposed to stilted world views.

Blame is best seen as a phase of the learning process. It can be accepted or rejected by the teacher or trainer. By accepting the feelings of Blame or Anger (as opposed to agreeing with the substance of the assertions), the teacher will help a student move on to the next phase. Rejecting the feelings ("Oh, don't be silly, no one did this deliberately. There's no conspiracy.") often encourages the student to stay stuck in the stage.

Self-Blame

When feelings of Blame are accepted, students typically progress to the third stage, Self-Blame: "I can't believe I've been so gullible!" "How come I've never known this before? What a dummy I've been."

Again, the teacher's acceptance of a student's feelings supports a healthy progression through the stage. Rejection of the feelings can result in a student's remaining stuck in this stage. With proper facilitation, students can move through all the stages, up to Problem-Solving, in a matter of hours or less.

Problem-Solving

In the final stage, Problem-Solving, the new reality is integrated into the learner's world view. In the case of the Peters, this means the construction of a new world view in which countries and continents have the areal proportions they actually have on the earth. Students are then ready to use this new world view as a component of their global awareness.

This DBSP process, which we have observed time and again, requires the teacher to be sensitive to the fact that the Peters image will radically challenge adult students' views of the world. Pushing the image on the group, on the other hand, will often only stimulate further discomfort and resistance to learning.

Kurt Lewin, the well-known social psychologist, developed a field theory for human behavior. One of Lewin's contentions was that if you want to change people's view of the world, the least effective strategy is to persist in insisting that your view is the superior one. Instead, Lewin recommends that to influence a change in a person's belief systems, the best approach is to fully appreciate and listen to the other person's world view and the reasons for it.

Only when one discovers why it is that another is so committed to a viewpoint can one respond to the specific component beliefs and work to reduce the

120

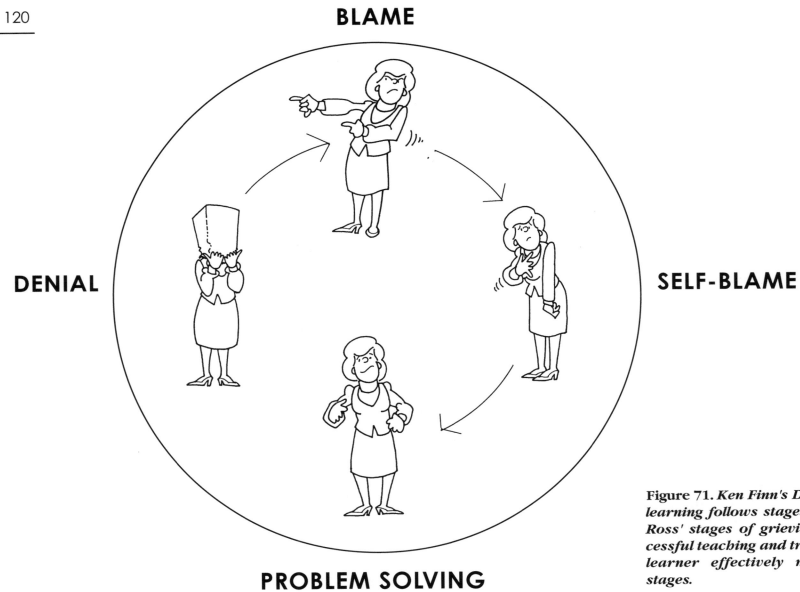

BLAME

DENIAL

SELF-BLAME

PROBLEM SOLVING

Figure 71. *Ken Finn's DBSP theory of adult learning follows stages similar to Kubler-Ross' stages of grieving. The key to successful teaching and training is to help the learner effectively move through the stages.*

Figure 72. *When two parties are in conflict, it is often more effective to encourage the other person to speak their mind than insist on getting your own point across. The negative cycle of arguing for one's own position is broken in panel #7 when the man gets an insight: "maybe by listening first, I will get a clearer picture of how this other person sees the world." One benefit to having nearly finished reading* Seeing Through Maps *is that you are surely convinced there are many different ways to see the world.*

122

other's commitment to those beliefs. The basic idea here is that it is easier to reduce resistance to change than to adhere dogmatically to an approach that tries to convince another person of the "rightness" of your viewpoint.

It is because map projections are all about view-point that they are so powerful in these educational settings.

The Peters Map in Action

The teacher or trainer using the Peters projection map ought to be prepared for strong emotional reactions. We have found that it is best to introduce the map as a different point of view, not a superior one. When people first see it and reject it out-of-hand, we recommend that the trainer not argue in its favor, but simply point out that it is an equal area projection.

One might even agree with objections, admitting that the Peters does significantly distort shape: "Yes, the Peters map doesn't show the world as it really is. You can only see that by looking at a globe." "Yes, if shape is your most important consideration, then the Peters image is terrible!" The teacher can slowly but surely, by recognizing and appreciating the arguments against the Peters projection, lead students to accept its validity as a tool for seeing sizes, proportions, even a broader view of the world.

Peter Bailey, the Global Business Solution Consultant at Wilson Learning Corporation, uses the Peters image in his company's custom training programs. One of Wilson Learning's client companies was a transnational telecommunications company which wanted to train its entire workforce of over 5,000 employees in a Global Effectiveness Program. The goals of the course were to encourage a global mindset and to teach people a global skill set.

Bailey says: "The Peters image was a wonderful tool in the classroom. It really helped people to shift their perspectives. We wanted people to grasp the idea that they needed to understand that people think, act, and communicate differently around the world. This may sound like a no-brainer, but this required a total shift in the thinking of both managers and employees. What works in Detroit doesn't necessarily work in Singapore or Buenos Aires. Company executives were required to switch from a U.S.-centric model to a globally expansive point of view. This applies to every aspect of organizational life. We're talking about different approaches to product launches, different ways to manage and conduct meetings, and different strategies for dealing with virtual team members from countries around the globe."

"A global perspective," says Bailey, "takes into consideration history, geography and politics. It includes considerations of national culture, sub-cultures (like gender, age, or business function), personal styles (like peoples' thinking styles), and corporate culture. Global business won't work with a cookie-cutter approach."

The Peters image helps to make these points ring true!

Michele Pendergraph is Assistant V.P. of Human Resources at Claims Administration Corporation in Rockville, Maryland. Pendergraph hired outside consultant Dianne LaMountain of Richmond, Virginia to run training programs using the Peters map. Pendergraph says: "It's as if you turned on a light bulb.

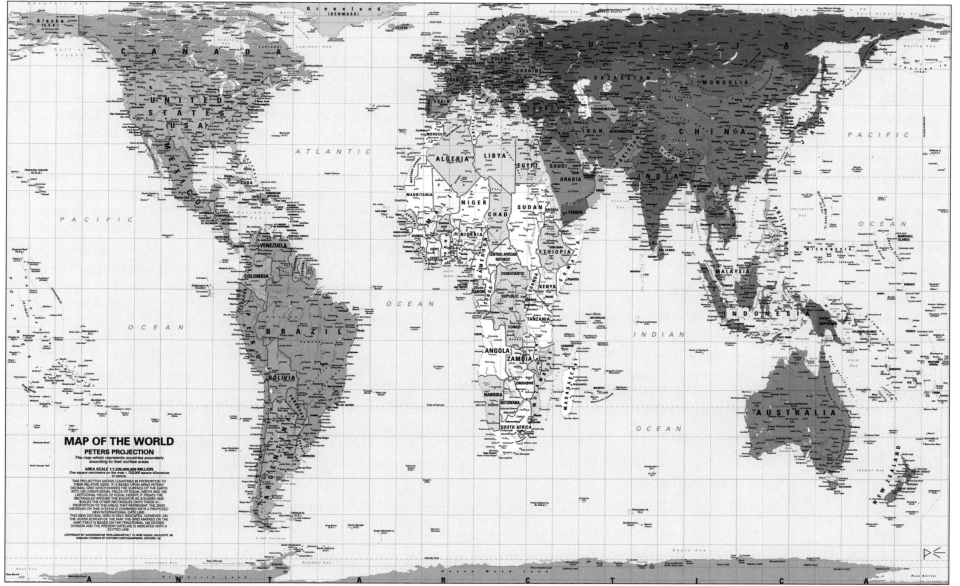

Figure 73. *This Peters projection map is used by many human resource development professionals as well as trainers and corporate culture change agents. It reinforces the point that the world may not be the way we thought it was. By illustrating this principle visually, adult learners who see the image become more open to learning other new concepts which help them adapt to organizational change and a turbulent business climate.*

124

[The Peters map] is very effective at getting people to think outside of the box."

LaMountain emphasizes three key lessons that can be drawn from the experience of the map: (1) it is critical to be aware of the various influences that have shaped our frame of reference and views of the world, (2) when we find ourselves thinking in terms of right and wrong it is important to explore whether, in fact, the points of view may just be different, and (3) it is important to seek out alternative sources of information on which to base our decisions. LaMountain says: "The map really helps to unfreeze peoples' minds, and open them up to new ways of seeing. It works to get them to see there are many ways to view the world."

Management consultant Bob Abramms of ODT (also the editor of this volume) has his own list of questions he finds helpful to ask when guiding seminar participants to discover the hidden meanings of maps.

What country do you think the mapmaker came from?

For what specific purposes do you think the map was created?

Who commissioned the map?

Who published the map?

Who buys the map?

What cultural assumptions or biases are reflected in the map?

What's at the center of the map?

What's relegated to the margins?

What's left off the map entirely?

What is the map about?

Does the map emphasize the needs and goals of the wealthiest class?

Are working class or community needs reflected in the map?

Are quality of life issues reflected? How about noise levels?

How might maps reflect things like air and water quality?

Does the map include the entire bioregion?

If not, what problems (upstream or downstream) might be hidden from our view?

How would you modify the map to better suit your needs and values?

Also: see the list of Questions in Chapter Three page 38

Map Projections and Other
Images of the World

PROJECTIONS

name	shape of the world	grid lines straignt?	right angles?	qualities	useful attributes	shows well	shows poorly
Aitoff 	True Ellipsoid	The equator and central line of longitude are straight; others are curved	They are more or less right-angled in the center of the projection, but elsewhere they are not	Compromise—neither equal area (does not show areas in true proportion) nor conformal (does not show shapes as they are on the globe)	Scale is constant (does not vary) along the equator and central line of longitude; varies elsewhere	Pleasing appearance for the world as a whole; shows the poles as points	Polar regions are compressed; shapes distorted towards edges
Azimuthal Equidistant	Circular	Except when a pole is in the center, most are curved	Only in special cases do angles form right angles in this projection	Equidistant (scale does not vary along lines drawn from the center of the map)	When a pole is in the center, lines of latitude are circles, and lines of longitude are straight	Scale is constant along any line drawn from the center of the map; shapes in center of map well represented	The farther from the center of the map, the greater the distortion
Boggs Eumorphic 	Oval (though the projection is typically shown interrupted, as here)	Lines of latitude are straight, lines of longitude are curved	They approximate to right angles, especially along central axes, but elsewhere they do not	Equal area	Averages properties of Mollweide and sinusoidal projections (compare to Goode's homolosine)	Sizes; also pretty good representation of large shapes, such as continents ("eumorphic" means "good shape")	Oceans, which in the typical interrupted form (shown here), are broken up

125

projection	shape	grid lines	angles	qualities	attributes	well	poorly
Collignon	Triangular	All lines of latitude and longitude are straight lines	Lines of latitude form right angles with central line of longitude; others are not right angles	Equal area		Sizes; but little else—this is a mathematical novelty: the projection shows that you can project the earth's surface into any shape	Almost everything shows poorly—for example the South Pole is a *line* nearly 1.5 times the length of the Equator (in fact, the South Pole is a point)
Eckert II	Hexagonal	All lines of latitude and longitude are straight lines	Lines of latitude form right angles with central line of longitude; others are not right angles	Equal area	Lines of latitude are straight lines; lines of longitude are broken straight lines	Sizes; but little else	Both poles are lines (in fact, both poles are points); shapes of equatorial regions are weirdly distorted
Eckert IV	Somewhat flattened oval	Lines of latitude are straight, lines of longitude are curved (actually, segments of ellipses)	Lines of latitude form right angles with central line of longitude; others approximate to right angles but are not	Equal area	Presents shapes comparatively well for an equal area projection	Sizes; shapes are comparatively good; makes a pleasing shape overall	Tropical regions are elongated in a north-south direction
Fuller Dymaxion	Cuboctahedron (six squares, eight triangles) or icosahedron (20 triangles)	Some are straight for a portion of the map, others curved	A few angles are right, but most are not	Compromise	Scale is constant along the *edges* of the polygons making up the projection	Shows shapes and sizes relatively well within each section of the map; also shows that we don't have to think about the world the way we usually do	Continuity of the earth is completely obliterated; distances and directions are almost impossible to make out

projection	shape	grid lines	angles	qualities	attributes	well	poorly
Gall's Orthographic (Gall-Peters or Peters) 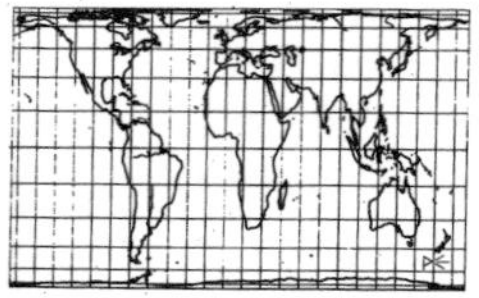	Rectangular	All grid lines are straight	The grid lines form right angles	Equal area	All lines of latitude and longitude are straight lines	Sizes	Shapes are significantly distorted every-where except at 45° north and south; tropical areas are stretched north and south; polar areas are compressed north and south
Goode's Homolosine 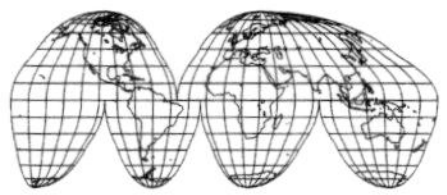	Interrupted	Grid resembles that of the sinusoidal (see below) from the Equator out to 40°, and that of Mollweide (see below) from 40° to the poles	Lines of latitude form right angles with the center line of longitude in each of the lobes	Equal area	Fusion of Mollweide (poleward part) and sinusoidal (equatorial part) —compare Boggs Eumorphic	Sizes; shapes are well represented within each lobe (except for Asia which is the most distorted continent)	Asia is not well represented; in typical interrupted form (shown here), oceans are broken up
Hammer 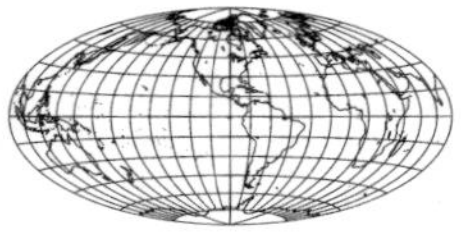	True Ellipsoid	Equator and central line of longitude are straight; all others are curved	Equator and central line of longitude make right angles, which others approximate less and less toward the poles	Equal area	Pleasing appearance for globe as a whole	Sizes; shapes in center of projection	The polar regions are compressed (as with most equal area projections), but there is less shearing than usual
Lambert's Cylindrical 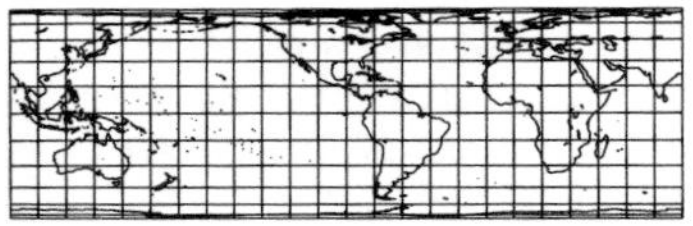	Rectangular	All grid lines are straight	The grid lines form right angles	Equal area	All lines of latitude and longitude are straight lines	Sizes; the shapes of places athwart the equator are good (displays Africa especially well)	Severe compression toward the poles

projection	shape	grid lines	angles	qualities	attributes	well	poorly
Mercator	Rectangular	All grid lines are straight	The grid lines form right angles	Conformal (shows true shapes, though only locally)	All lines of latitude and longitude are straight lines; all straight lines are lines of constant compass bearing (good for navigation)	Compass bearings; shapes are true for small regions of the globe (good for making maps of local areas)	Cannot represent the poles at all; sizes are radically exaggerated poleward of the equator; because of scale variation, shapes are true only locally
Mollweide	True Ellipsoid	The central line of longitude and all lines of latitude are straight; others are curved (segments of ellipses)	Lines of latitude cross the central line of longitude at right angles; others approximate to right angles, though less and less the farther you get from the center	Equal area	Lines of latitude are straight	Sizes; shapes in center of projection	The polar regions are compressed (as with most equal area projections), but there is less shearing than often
Peters (also known as the Gall-Peters or Gall Orthographic)	Rectangular	All grid lines are straight	The grid lines form right angles	Equal area	All lines of latitude and longitude are straight lines	Sizes	Shapes are significantly distorted everywhere except at 45° north and south; tropical areas are stretched north and south; polar areas are compressed north and south
Robinson	Sort of oval, except the poles are represented by lines	Equator and all lines of latitude are straight; others curved	Lines of latitude make right angles with central line of longitude	Compromise	Presents a very pleasing image of the globe	Shapes are pretty good, especially in the equatorial region (used by the National Geographic Society for its world maps from 1988 to 1998)	Poles are straight lines (though in fact they are points); areas away from equator are exaggerated in size

projection	shape	grid lines	angles	qualities	attributes	well	poorly
Sinusoidal (often called the Sanson or Sanson-Flamsteed after early users) 	Sinusoidal	The central line of longitude and all lines of latitude are straight; others are curved (cosine curves)	Only the lines of latitude crossing the central line of longitude make right angles; all others are more or less acute	Equal area	Lines of latitude are straight and evenly spaced; scale is true along each line of latitude and central line of longitude	Areas near center of image	Areas along edges of map are considerably distorted, especially toward the poles
Van der Grinten (specifically, Van der Grinten I) 	Circular (maps made in this projection usually delete the polar regions, so they appear rectangular	Equator and central line of longitude are straight; all others are curved (arcs of circles)	Equator and central line of longitude form right angle; others do not	Compromise	Retains familiar appearance of the Mercator, but with reduced areal distortion	Shapes in central portion are well represented (used by the National Geographic Society for its world maps for most of the last century)	Although less than Mercator, regions toward the poles are significantly exaggerated in size; distortion of the actual polar regions is so great they are rarely shown
Winkel Tripel	Sort of oval, except the poles are represented by lines	Equator and central line of longitude are straight, lines of latitude are gently curved, lines of longitude are curved more sharply	Angles in the central region of the map approximate to right	Compromise	Resembles Robinson in presenting a pleasing image of the globe, but areal exaggeration is less toward the poles	Shapes are fairly well represented; sizes are not equivalent, but exaggeration is not extreme (currently used by the National Geographic Society for its world maps)	The farther from the center of the map (Africa, South America) the greater the distortion; poles are lines (in fact they are points)

OTHER WORLD MAPS

name	shape	grid lines	angles	qualities	attributes	well	poorly
Guelke's Map Centered on Toronto	Circular	Center line is straight, all others curved	Grid makes no right angles	Equidistant	This is an azimuthal equidistant projection specifically centered on Toronto. Great for comparing distances from Toronto to all other places on the map	Scale is constant along any line drawn from the center of the map; shapes in center of map well represented	The farther from the center of the map, the greater the distortion
McArthur's Universal Corrective Map of the World	Rectangular	All grid lines are straight	The grid lines form right angles	Compromise	Map is oriented with south at the top, and with Australia in the center, resulting in an "unusual" view of the world	The cylindrical stereographic projection is especially appropriate given the prominence of Australia and the Pacific which are quite well represented	Polar regions are extremely distorted in this projection; indeed, they are not shown on this map at all
Van Sant's Maps	Various	Depends on the projection used; the one used in this book uses the Robinson (see above)	Depends on the projection used; the one used in this book uses the Robinson (see above)	Various	Brilliantly realized images of the whole planet or selected continents, meticulously composed from hundreds of millions of satellite images	Physiography (mountains and valleys) and natural vegetation are clearly displayed	Human culture (national boundaries, distributions of languages, religions, and so on) are not shown at all

name	shape	grid lines	angles	qualities	attributes	well	poorly
What's Up? South! World Map 	Rectangular cropping of Van der Grinten projection	Equator and central line of longitude are straight; all others are curved (arcs of circles)	Equator and central line of longitude form right angle; others do not	Compromise; orientation reversed; south on top	Demonstrates that North does not equal "up"	Provocative; challenges assumptions; shapes in central portion are well represented	Although less than Mercator, regions toward the poles are significantly exaggerated in size; distortion of the actual polar regions is so great they are cropped off

Note: This chart includes most of the map projections treated in the text arranged in alphabetical order. Following the projections are a few other images of the world we discuss.

In charts like this one, map projections are often classified by how they are made. We have not done this, since we do not believe this is important for most users. Instead, we have included information useful for answering the questions we raised the closing pages of Chapter Three.

The projections are described in their normal aspect, that is, as they are usually seen and used in maps of the world.

LIST OF ILLUSTRATIONS

[NOTE: Sources in **bold** are commercially available from various publishers]

Frontage p. i **Globe imagery** supplied by **Oxford Cartographers**, Oasis Park, Eynsham, Oxford OX29 4TP, UK. **Tel +44 (0)1865 882 884 Fax +44 (0) 1865 882925** Website: **www.oxfordcarto.com**

1. *Duke guard's map*. Courtesy of the collection of Denis Wood.

2. *The Mercator projection*. From *Map Projections: A Working Manual*, John P. Snyder, USGS Professional Paper 1395, 1987, Washington D.C. (p. 40). A **Mercator Projection** similar to the illustration on the cover of this book is available from **ODT, Inc. (1-800-736-1293; www.diversophy.com/maps.htm; Fax: 413-549-3503; Email: seeingmaps@aol.com)**.

3. *Mercator's map*. Drawn by Roy Collins in Wellman Chamberlin's *The Round Earth on Flat Paper*, National Geographic Society, 1947, 1950. Washington D.C. *(p.s 80-81)*.

4. *Areal distortion on Mercator's projection*. From **A New View of the World**, **Ward L. Kaiser**, Friendship Press (New York, NY) and ODT, Inc. (Amherst MA); 1987, 1993. (p. 12).

5. *Comparison of a rhumb line and a great circle route*. From **Elements of Cartography**, **Robinson et. al.**, **5th edition**, John Wiley & Sons, Copyright 1984, p. 84. (**1-800-225-5945**; Fax: 1-732-302-2300)

6. **The Peters projection**. From *The New Cartography*, Arno Peters, Friendship Press, NY, NY, 1983, (p. 125). Map available from **ODT, Inc. (1-800-736-1293 ; www.petersmap.com Fax: 413-549-3503; Email: petersmaps@aol.com)**.

7. *The human face on four different projections*. ODT, Inc., Amherst MA, 2001. Reproduction rights available from 1-800-736-1293 (petersmaps@aol.com).

8. *A map in a sketch drawn in a game of Pictionary*. Courtesy of the collection of Denis Wood.

9. *A Duke student draws the world*. Courtesy of the collection of Denis Wood.

10. *A medieval European plan of the world*. From *Rudimentum Novitiorum*, Lubeck, 1475.

11. *Projecting the world onto a plane*. From *The New Cartography*, Arno Peters, Friendship Press, NY, NY, 1983, (p. 81).

12. *The graticule*. From *Map Projections: A Working Manual*, John P. Snyder, USGS Professional Paper 1395, 1987, Washington D.C. (p. 9).

13. *Gores*. From **Flattening the Earth**, **John P. Snyder**, University of Chicago Press, 1997, Chicago IL (p. 42).

14. *Goode's homosoline*. From *Map Projections: A Working Manual*, John P. Snyder, USGS Professional Paper 1395, 1987, Washington D.C. (p. 197).

15. *Gall's Orthographic Projection*. From **Flattening the Earth**, **John P. Snyder**, University of Chicago Press, 1997, Chicago IL (p. 108).

16. *Lambert's cylindrical equal-area projection*. From *An Album of Map Projections*, John P. Snyder, USGS Professional Paper 1453; 1989, 1994, Washington D.C. (p. 17).

17. *Lambert's cylindrical equal-area projection of Africa*. From **Flattening the Earth**, **John P. Snyder**, University of Chicago Press, 1997, Chicago IL (p. 86).

18. *Six equal-area projections*.

   Sinusoidal. From *An Album of Map Projections*, John P. Snyder, USGS Professional Paper 1453: 1989, 1994, Washington D.C. (p. 17).
   Mollweide. From *An Album of Map Projections*, John P. Snyder, USGS Professional Paper 1453: 1989, 1994, Washington D.C. (p. 55).
   Hammer. From *An Album of Map Projections*, John P. Snyder, USGS Professional Paper 1453: 1989, 1994, Washington D.C. (p. 161).
   Eckert II. From *An Album of Map Projections*, John P. Snyder, USGS Professional Paper 1453: 1989, 1994, Washington D.C. (p. 89).
   Eckert IV. From *An Album of Map Projections*, John P. Snyder, USGS Professional Paper 1453: 1989, 1994, Washington D.C. (p. 61).
   Boggs eumorphic. From **Flattening the Earth**, **John P. Snyder**, University of Chicago Press, 1997, Chicago, IL, (p. 200).

19. *Collignon's equal-area projection*. From *An Album of Map Projections*, John P. Snyder, USGS Professional Paper 1453: 1989, 1994, Wash. D.C. (p. 85).

20. *Guelke's Azimuthal Equidistant Projection*. Courtesy of the collection of Ward L. Kaiser. Originally published as a poster, *It's Your World Toronto*, Leonard Guelke, Currently out-of-print but a free download is available from www.diversophy.com/Guelke.htm

21. **Arno Peters' Projection of the World. Source of map: see #6 above.**

22. *Mercator's Projection of the World*. From *Map Projections: A Working Manual*, John P. Snyder, USGS Professional Paper 1395, 1987, Wash. D.C. (p. 40).

23. *Activity Page*. Copyright-free. Compliments of ODT, Inc.

24. *Andrew Kent's hand drawn map of the world.* Courtesy of the collection of Ward L. Kaiser.

25. *Jessica Kim's hand drawn map of the world.* Courtesy of the collection of Ward L. Kaiser.

26. **Buckminster Fuller's Dymaxion World Map**. © The Buckminster Fuller Institute, 111 N. Main Street, Sebastopol CA 94572; **707-824-2242; www.bfi.org**

27. *Continuous and interrupted maps,*
   Mollweide. From *An Album of Map Projections*, John P. Snyder, USGS Professional Paper 1453: 1989, 1994, Washington D.C. (p. 55).
   Goode's. From **Flattening the Earth**, **John P. Snyder**, University of Chicago Press, 1997, Chicago, IL, (p. 197).

28. *Different shaped maps.*
   Mercator. From *Map Projections: A Working Manual*, John P. Snyder, USGS Professional Paper 1395, 1987, Washington D.C. (p. 40).
   Sinusoidal. From *An Album of Map Projections*, John P. Snyder, USGS Professional Paper 1453: 1989, 1994, Washington D.C. (p. 38).
   Eckert II. From *An Album of Map Projections*, John P. Snyder, USGS Professional Paper 1453: 1989, 1994, Washington D.C. (p. 89).
   Eckert IV. From *An Album of Map Projections*, John P. Snyder, USGS Professional Paper 1453: 1989, 1994, Washington D.C. (p. 61).
   Collignon's. From *An Album of Map Projections*, John P. Snyder, USGS Professional Paper 1453: 1989, 1994, Washington D.C. (p. 85).
   Guelke's. From the collection of Ward L. Kaiser. A free dowload is available from www.diversophy.com/Guelke.htm

29. *Graticule* From *Map Projections: A Working Manual*, John P. Snyder, USGS Professional Paper 1395, 1987, Washington D.C. (p. 9).

30. *Mercator and sinusoidal; Mercator* (see #2 above); *Sinusoidal* (see #18 above)

31. *The Mercator and the Gall-Peters. Mercator* (see #2 above); *Peters* (see #6 above)

32. *The* **three official National Geographic Society maps** *in one comparative frame.* Adapted with permission from **The Nystrom Desk Atlas**, 1999 edition, p.s 138 - 139. Available from **Nystrom, 3333 Elston Avenue, Chicago IL 60618 (1-800-621-8086)**.

33. **The USA as Seen from Canada**. Part of the Global Perspective Series created by Russell H. Lenz. Available from **World Eagle, 111 King Street, Littleton MA 01460-1527; 1-800-854-8273; 1-978-486-9180; www.worldeagle.com; Fx: 978-486-9652; Email: info@WorldEagle.com**

34. *An Isidore-type map from 1472.* From **Flattening the Earth**, **John P. Snyder**, University of Chicago Press, 1997, Chicago IL (p. 2).

35. **The "What's Up? South!" World Map**. From **ODT, Inc. (1-800-736-1293; www.seeingmaps.com; Fax: 413-549-3503; Email: seeingmaps@aol.com)**. Also available at local map and book stores.

36. *Fragment of a scale map of Rome.* From *The History of Topographical Maps*, P.D.A. Harvey. Thames and Hudson, London, 1980, *p.* 129. Museo Capitolino, Rome.

37. *Erhard Etzlaub's 1501 map of central Europe.* From *The History of Topographical Maps*, P.D.A. Harvey. Thames and Hudson, London, 1980, *p.* 148. By permission of the Houghton Library, Harvard University, MRH N 2.

38. *The Van der Grinten projection.* From *An Album of Map Projections*, John P. Snyder, USGS Professional Paper, 1453: 1989, 1994, Wash. D.C. (p. 201).

39. **McArthur's Universal Corrective Map of the World**. In the Americas and Europe, available from **ODT, Inc.; (1-800-736-1293; www.seeingmaps.com; Fax: 413-549-3503; Email: seeingmaps@aol.com)**
   In Australia, Asia, and Africa available from **Rex Publications, 22 Alto Ave., North Seaforth NSW 2092, Australia; 011-612-994-85399; FAX: 011-612-994-85397; Email: JimBow@smartchat.com.au**.

40. *A polar Lambert azimuthal equal-area projection.* From *An Album of Map Projections*, John P. Snyder, USGS Professional Paper 1453: 1989, 1994, Washington D.C. (p. 137).

41. *Robinson.* From *An Album of Map Projections*, John P. Snyder, USGS Professional Paper 1453: 1989, 1994, Washington D.C. (p. 83).

42. *The Winkel Tripel.* From *An Album of Map Projections*, John P. Snyder, USGS Professional Paper 1453: 1989, 1994, Washington D.C. (p. 165).

43. *The human face on four different projections.* See #7 above.

44. *Greenland on the three compromise projections.* All images taken from *An Album of Map Projections*, John P. Snyder, USGS Professional Paper 1453: 1989, 1994, Washington D.C. (p.s 201, 83, 165).

45. *The equirectangular projection.* From *An Album of Map Projections*, John P. Snyder, USGS Professional Paper 1453: 1989, 1994, Wash. D.C. (p. 23).

46. *The azimuthal equidistant projection.* From **Flattening the Earth**, **John P. Snyder**, University of Chicago Press, 1997, Chicago IL (p. 30).

47. *The Aitoff projection.* From *An Album of Map Projections*, John P. Snyder, USGS Professional Paper 1453: 1989, 1994, Washington D.C. (p. 159).

48. *The Winkel Tripel.* From *An Album of Map Projections*, John P. Snyder, USGS Professional Paper 1453: 1989, 1994, Washington D.C. (p. 165).

49. **Tom Van Sant's map of the world**. © The GeoSphere Project / Tom Van Sant. Order from **www.geosphere.com** or **1-800-845-1522**.

50. *Hockney photocollage.* Billy Wilder Lighting His Cigar, Dec 1982, Photographic Collage, Ed: 20, 27 X 17.5", © David Hockney.

51. *Earth rising over the moon.* Photo courtesy of NASA.

52. *Three interrupted projections.*
> *Sinusoidal.* From *An Album of Map Projections,* John P. Snyder, USGS Professional Paper 1453: 1989, 1994, Washington D.C. (p. 43).
> *Goode's interrupted Mollweide.* From **Flattening the Earth, John P. Snyder,** University of Chicago Press, 1997, Chicago IL (p. 168).
> *Goode's homolosine.* From *An Album of Map Projections,* John P. Snyder, USGS Prof. Paper 1453: 1989, 1994, Washington D.C. (p. 67).

53. *Robinson's projection.* See #41 above.

54. *An image of the earth with ... clouds.* From Claire Parkinson's *Earth from Above: Using Color-Coded Satellite Images to Examine the Global Environment* (University Science Books, 55D Gate Five Road, Sausalito, CA, 94965), p. 3.

55. *The earth at night.* Courtesy of http://antwrp.gsfc.nasa.gov/apod/ap001127.html. The image is downloadable at http://antwrp.gsfc.nasa.gov/apod/image/ap0011/earthlights_dmsp_big.jpg

56. *A map indicating the changing seasons.* This "Hardiness Zones" map is from Gurney's Seed & Nursery Co. supplied to customers in their *2001 Spring Catalog.* It is a public domain image from the U.S. Department of Agriculture.

57. **Minard's map of Napoleon's invasion of Russia.** This is a re-creation of Minard's map. This English version is available from **ODT, Inc. (1-800-736-1293).** The original was in French. A poster of the original version is available from **Graphics Press, Box 430, Cheshire, Connecticut 06410.** The French version can also be found in **The Visual Display of Quantitative Information, Edward Tufte, Graphics Press, 1983,** p. 41).

58. **Petit's map of the slave trade.** From **The Penguin Atlas of Diasporas, Gérard Chaliand & Jean-Pierre Rageau, Penguin-Viking, NY, 1995** (p. 114).

59. *Beck's map of the London Underground* from Ken Garland's *Mr Beck's Underground Map,* published in 1994 by Capital Transport, 38 Long Elmes, Harrow Weald, Middlesex. © London Underground Limited. All rights reserved.

60. **A cartogram showing the population of each country.** Available in poster form (Item #: 12-391) from **Poster Education, P.O. Box 8696, Asheville, NC 28732; 800-858-0969.** On the web at **www.postereducation.com.** (A lesson plan is also available as part of Global Studies Kit #10-6347)

61. *Global Warming cartogram.* From the **State of the World Atlas,** Dan Smith, pp. 98-99, Penguin Books Limited. Copyright © 1999, Myriad Editions Ltd All rights reserved. For info contact: **www.MyriadEditions.com**

62. *Clip art of clockface.*

63. *Equidistant map.* Toronto-centered by Guelke. Free download available from www.diversophy.com/Guelke.htm

64. *Babylonian map.* From *The New Cartography,* Arno Peters, Friendship Press, New York, NY, 1983, (p. 12).

65. *Al Idrisi.* From *The New Cartography,* Arno Peters, Friendship Press, New York, NY, 1983, (p. 28).

66. *Tokyo-centered map of the world.* Out of print. Publisher is at 011-81-3(404)4461.

67. *Martin Behaim.* From John Fiske, *Globe in Mercator Projection,* 1902.

68. *Photos* courtesy of the Berkshire Design Group; Northampton MA; 413-582-7000; www.BerkshireDesign.com

69. **X-ray eyes.** Cartoon courtesy of ODT, Inc. © 2001. All rights reserved.

70. *Clip art of eye.*

71. **The DBSP cycle.** Cartoon courtesy of ODT, Inc. © 2001. All rights reserved.

72. **The Listening Process.** Cartoon courtesy of ODT, Inc. © 2001. All rights reserved.

73. **Peters Projection Map.** Courtesy of Friendship Press. © Akademische Verlagsanstalt. Single copy reproduction rights granted to individuals and non-profit organizations. Others call 800-736-1293.

Illustration from front cover: *The Mercator projection.* See entry #2 above

Illustrations from back cover (clockwise from top left):
> A. *The Mercator projection.* See entry #2 above
> B. *The earth from space.* Photo courtesy of NASA.
> C. *Population cartogram.* See entry #60 above.
> D. *"What's Up? South!" world map.* See entry #33 above.
> E. *Oxford globe.* See entry #i above.
> F. *Peters projection.* See entry #6 above.
> G. *Fuller Dymaxion projection.* See entry #26 above.

Meeting and event planners, administrators, and conference coordinators:

Discuss your needs
for your next training session,
in-service program or keynote

135

CONTACT 1-800-736-1293

What we offer:

Teacher Training
Seminars & Workshops
In-service Training
Keynote Speeches
University Symposia
"Honor the Earth" Celebrations
"Green" Events
Train-the-trainer

Topics include:

New Mental Map Workshops

Seeing Through Maps Programs

Peters Projection Seminars

Managing Diversity

Exposing the **Hidden Agenda** of Maps

Contemporary Cartographic Controversies

FUN-damentals of Cartography

The Power of Maps as a Force for Change

Mapping Your Way to a High Performance Team

Maps as Windows on the **Soul**

The **Myth** of the Objective Map

Bring a new way of looking at the world to your organization!
Stimulate innovative thinking!
Help your staff to "think outside the box."
A professional **rejuvenation!**

Mention this ad and code
STM901 and **get $100 worth**
of map products when you
book your next event!

For:
Corporate
Non-profit
Public Sector
Community Events
Religious Festivals

Please copy this form to share with your friends!

SEEING THROUGH MAPS Order Form

Kaiser
...s Wood
$19.95

Tell your friends they can
Download Chapter One
FREE
at
www.diversophy.com/maps.htm

Special discounts for bulk purchases for sales promotions, premiums, fund-raising or educational use
Contact: Director, Special Markets, ODT, Inc: 1-800-736-1293; 1-413-549-1327; Fax: 1-413-549-3503; E-mail: seeingmaps@aol.com

❏ Yes! Please send me_____copy(ies) of **SEEING THROUGH MAPS: The Power of Images to Shape Our World View** at $19.95 each.................**Book Total** =_____

❏ Yes! I want other items (please attach list)...**Other Items Total** =_____

Shipping and Handling is $5.50 for first book/item, $1.25 each for additional books/items on your order..**S&H Total** =_____

MA Residents add 5% tax (or provide tax-exempt number_____)..............**Tax Total** =_____

❏ Prepaid order. Check enclosed, check#_____

❏ Charge to my MC/Visa/Amex account number_____ EXP Date:_____   **Grand Total** =_____

❏ Bill me (purchase order or request on company letterhead required) PURCHASE ORDER#_____

Name_____Title_____
                                   (please print)

Organization_____

Street Address (no P.O. Boxes)_____

City_____State_____Zip (Postal Code)_____Phone (required) (_____)_____

ODT, Inc.
P.O. Box 134
Amherst, MA 01004

CALL Toll-Free 1-800-736-1293   **FAX** your order to (413) 549-350

Standard **Peters Map Teacher's Package**—$39 plus $5.50 shipping
includes one each of the following:
- Laminated Peters Projection Wall Map (35"x51")
- Laminated Peters Mini-map (11"x17")
- *A New View of the World* (which explains a variety
  of cartographic approaches and principles, along with
  the key message of fairness in the Peters Map)
- Peters Postcard

Peters Map **Corporate Seminar Pack**- $149 plus $9.50 shipping
includes:
- Everything from the standard and deluxe packages
- User's Guide to maximize training impact
- **Fully reproducible** 4-page Peters Map handout
- **Fully reproducible** handout for diversity training
- One additional laminated Peters Mini-map
- "Rock Your World" from *Training & Development*
- "Our View of the World" from *Take a Walk in My Shoes*
- All three wall maps come in durable see-through tubes
- Two Peters Map refrigerator magnets (for prizes)
- **BONUS!** 24 Peters Map Postcards—great way to
  reinforce the message and have students take it home!

Deluxe Peters Map Trainer's Package—$89 plus **$6.50 shipping**
includes:
- The standard $39 Trainer's Package
- Two additional laminated wall maps for comparison purposes:
  —the standard Mercator Projection (34" x 52")
  —the **"What's Up? South!"** World Map—
  Van der Grinten Projection

Call Toll-Free 1-800-736-1293 or visit www.diversophy.com/maps.htm

137

Map Resources

PETERS PROJECTION WALL MAP

35"x50" paper full-color wall map;
includes eight informational panels.
Folds to 8 ½" x 12"
Each country shown at true size.
Includes a 4-page Explanation.

$20.00

WHAT'S UP? SOUTH! WORLD MAP

The world from a different perspective.
South on top. Paper. 36" x 56"
Van der Grinten Projection.
Folds to 9 ½"x 11 ¾".
Includes a 4-page Explanation.

$20.00

A NEW VIEW OF THE WORLD

Popular handbook explains the
principles behind Peters Projection in detail.
Chapter on hidden messages maps send.
(42 pages, perfect bound)

$7.00

PETERS PROJECTION MINI-MAP

Full-color paper 11"X 17" with explanation
on back.

$6.00

NEW MENTAL MAP PACKET

One 1990 Peters mini-map;
New View *booklet: eight data*
panels; Earth stickers: six Peters
postcards and the unique
SELF-ESTEEM PASSPORT.

while supplies last

$18.00

PETERS MAP REFRIGERATOR MAGNET

A 4"x6" oversized magnet
with sturdy 10 mil lamination.
Intrigue your guests
with this great visual aid.

$5.00

SEEING THROUGH MAPS FILE CABINET MAGNET

A huge 6" x 9" oversized magnet with
sturdy 10 mil lamination. Same quiz as STM
postcard. Great office conversation piece!
Special 1/2 price offer: buy 5 get 5 free: only $37.50

$7.50

PETERS PROJECTION PRESENTATION RESOURCES

A set of 14 overhead transparencies
or 35mm slides used by presenters
and trainers to teach the lessons
of the Peters Projection Map.
Organizational License Included!

$250.00

MERCATOR PROJECTION MAP

"Traditional" or standard map projection
(34"x 52"; centered on North America);
in durable plastic tube. No explanation.

$29.95

USA shipping and handling charges: $5.50 for 1st item, $1.25 each additional item. For Canada and other international rates contact petersmaps@aol.com or 800-736-1293

139

164 Pages

128 Pages

Complimentary Book With Any Order Over $25

Your choice of one of these outstanding books

(While Supplies Last)

Available ONLY with credit card phone orders. Call 1-800-736-1293 Mention code: STM 901
Shipping and handling on the free book is only $1.25 additional

370 Pages

208 Pages

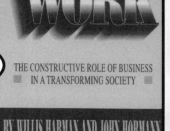

Cultural Diversity Fieldbook:
Fresh Visions & Breakthrough Strategies for Revitalizing the Workplace.

120 of today's most provocative voices speak their minds on Race, Class and Diversity Under Fire. Activities, facts, resource lists, poetry, dramatic dialog.

Cultural Diversity:
A Workshop for Trainers

Two experienced diversity trainers show others in their field how to maximize productivity and reduce the challenges of a multi-cultural workforce. All the *basic building blocks* of diversity training are revealed. Three ring binder

273 Pages
8" x 8"
$27

248 Pages
REPRODUCTION RIGHTS INCLUDED!
$100

360 Pages
REPRODUCTION RIGHTS INCLUDED
$125

6 Pages
$30.00 per pack of ten tipsheets

Diversity Awareness Resources

ODT's Training & Development products have won numerous **national awards**.

Like our diverse map products, these resources will expand your horizons and stimulate your thinking.

These are samples of what we offer...

we'll be glad to tell you more...*800-736-1293*

The Questions of Diversity

An assessment process for diversity initiatives. A comprehensive and easy to use collection of techniques, instruments, case studies, tips, quizzes, articles and a *high powered* **In Basket** activity. Includes computer disk for easy customization. Three ring binder with Microsoft Word 7.0 disk. Seventh Edition

Working with People
from Diverse Backgrounds

Six-page tipsheet includes informative look at differences in cultural values: racial vs. ethnic identity; issues of immigration and acculturation; plus how to be more successful in a multicultural environment. Use as an ice-breaking activity. Heavy card stock.

For a closer look at our full line of diversity awareness training and development products see

Index

Bold type (e.g. **101**) indicates figure/caption sitation

ABOUT THE AUTHORS:

Featured on Ira Glass's *This American Life*, **Denis Wood** is one of America's best-loved experts on the significance and meaning of maps. Wood loves maps and loves to talk about them. Besides *Seeing Through Maps*, Wood is the author of the best-selling *The Power of Maps*. He also curated the award-winning exhibition of maps at the Cooper-Hewitt National Design Museum in 1992, and its even more popular incarnation at the Smithsonian in Washington the year after.

A writer/artist, Wood is also a social scientist. He has published over 60 articles in a variety of journals that range from *Industrialization Forum* to *The Journal of Environmental Psychology*. During the '70s, Wood co-authored the best-selling *World Geography Today*, and in the '90s the respected *Home Rules*. His *Five Billion Years of Global Change* will be published by Guilford Press.

Dr. Wood earned his Ph.D. and Masters in geography from Clark University, a school with a geography program that is among the most highly regarded in the USA. His undergraduate degree, in English, is from Case Western Reserve in Cleveland, Ohio, where Wood grew up. From 1996 to 1998 Wood served two years in prison. Wood's book about that experience, *Soft Time in a Hard Place*, was commissioned by John Hopkins University Press. It will be published in 2002.

A former educator, Wood taught high school in Worcester, Massachusetts. Later he taught environmental psychology and landscape history for nearly a quarter of a century in the School of Design at North Carolina State University. During the '90s he was simultaneously a visiting professor at Duke University in the international studies program.

He has lectured around the world. In 1995 he keynoted the annual meeting of the North American Cartographic Information Society. His consulting clients have ranged from Esselte Map Services and Maple Lake Sports Camps to Merrill Lynch and Manufacturers Hanover Trust .

Ward Kaiser has broad experience as a publisher, ecumenical executive, pastor, teacher and community organizer. He introduced the Peters Projection world map to North America, publishing its first English-language version in 1983. His handbook to that map, *A New View of the World*, "the most effective piece of writing that has come out concerning the Peters Projection," is widely used by high school and college teachers, mission educators and social activists.

National Public Radio, NBC-TV, CBC-Radio and -Television, Vision TV as well as many local media outlets in Canada and the United States have had Kaiser as a guest. He has lectured extensively at colleges and universities and led worldview workshops and professional development seminars. Even in "retirement" he maintains a busy schedule of lecturing and writing.

Kaiser has also translated or co-translated several works on cartography into English. His editorial and publishing background continues to be called upon through consulting services to several publishing enterprises in Europe and the United States. This is Kaiser's sixth book.

A graduate of Wilfrid Laurier University, Waterloo, Ontario, and of Union Theological Seminary, New York, Kaiser has pursued further graduate studies in history, education, cultural anthropology, theology, economics and business administration. His volunteer work has included fair access to housing for all, Scouting and other youth programs, work with blind and visually handicapped persons, intercultural relations and political action for peace and justice. In his spare time he enjoys cycling. Recently, accompanied by his son, he completed a bike tour in France, following the same route—and using the same, well-worn Michelin map—he had taken 50 years earlier.

When not traveling, Kaiser and his wife, Lorraine, live in central Florida and the Niagara Peninsula of Ontario. Briefly British, then Canadian, now with dual American-Canadian citizenship, he strives to maintain an inclusive view as a world citizen. He may be reached at newmapper@aol.com or newmapper3@aol.com.

ABOUT THE EDITOR:

Dr. Bob Abramms is an international expert on designing, conducting and evaluating management training and executive development programs. Bob's background includes a B.S. in industrial engineering, Master's degrees in both business administration and counseling, and a doctorate in applied behavioral science. He has published five books and over fifty articles on leadership, motivation, human relations training, prejudice, stereotyping, and cultural differences. He has conducted seminars on "Managing Cultural Differences" for a wide variety of corporate and association clients.

ABOUT THE PUBLISHER:

ODT, Inc. is an employee-owned Massachusetts-based management consulting and publishing company focusing on topics of employee empowerment, performance appraisal and self-directed work teams. In 1990 ODT's *Complete Cultural Diversity Library* won an award as one of the year's "20 hottest Human Resource products."

ODT pioneered the use of the Peters Projection Map materials in large corporations and has been involved in using the map in a variety of corporate culture change, leadership and diversity diagnostic projects.

ODT's 1996-7 diversity trilogy won numerous awards: *The Cultural Diversity Fieldbook*—"Best Book Bet" by *Executive Female*; *The Cultural Diversity Sourcebook*—"Outstanding Book Award" by the Gustavus Myers Center for the Study of Human Rights in North America; and both books together won a "Top Training Product" award from *Human Resource Executive* magazine.

ODT has been the official marketing arm for the Peters Projection map since 1998. In February 2001, ODT granted permission to the TV show *West Wing* to feature the Peters Projection map in their award-winning series. Since then, ODT has grown beyond the boundaries of being simply a human resource consulting company. ODT's mission of "honoring differences" and "teaching people to see the world from a broader, more inclusive perspective" remain at the core of all our activities. Plans for the next five years include extensive in-service teacher training and train-the-trainer workshops to expand the reach of our message.

WEB RESOURCES

As a service to readers, the publisher is providing web resources to keep up-to-date materials available. The official web site for **Seeing Through Maps** is **www.seeingmaps.com**, which will be fully operational after 1/1/02.

The maps home page at George Simons International will provide access to teacher resources like learning objectives, quizzes, new applications and downloadable support materials. Visit: **www.diversophy.com/maps.htm**

You will also note that ODT has many map resources available at **www.petersmap.com**

If you have ideas and suggestions for web-based resources, or wish to contact the editor of **Seeing Through Maps**, contact BAbramms@aol.com

ANSWERS TO QUESTIONS ON THE BACK COVER

1.   Which image shows population sizes?

A cartogram is a map on which each country is shown with its size proportional to its population or some other attribute. Cartograms are used to show, among other things, measures of industrial output, oil consumption, wealth, and spending. They can give you a different perspective. More information is found on pages 86-89 See page 89 for a cartogram showing global warming concerns.

www.postereducation.com

2.   Which images shows how big each country is?

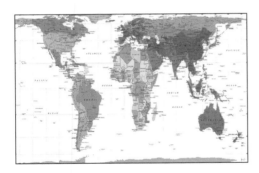

The Peters Projection Map is probably best known for being "fair to all peoples." Each country is shown in proportion to its actual size. But it looks weird! See pages 10, 32, 33, 46, 98, 122 and 123 for more information on the Peters. Other equal-area maps share this attribute of being true to size. See Goode's homolosine and the Mollweide projection on pages 25, 39 and 73. The Dymaxion Map™ (facing page, top right) is also an equal-area projection.

www.petersmap.com

3.   Which image shows "North" isn't the same as "up"?

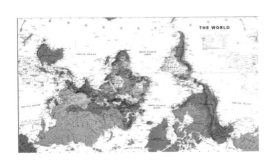

This a Van der Grinten projection (see page 49) with South on top. Who ever said that "North" is necessarily "up"? Up is over our heads, and it is only relatively recently that maps have been oriented to the North. In olden days maps were oriented to the East (and other directions as well). More on this can be found on pages 48-52.

www.seeingmaps.com